Books should be returned or renewed by the
last date stamped above

CHARTER
MARK

CUSTOMER SERVICE EXCELLENCE

Libraries & Archives

Kent
County
Council

This material was first published as hardback in 2004 by Bardfield Press
Bardfield Press is an imprint of Miles Kelly Publishing Ltd
Bardfield Centre, Great Bardfield, Essex, CM7 4SL

This edition published in 2006 by Miles Kelly Publishing Ltd

2 4 6 8 10 9 7 5 3 1

Editorial Director: Belinda Gallagher
Art Director: Jo Brewer
Volume Designer: Tom Slemmings
Cover Designer: Jo Brewer
Editorial Assistant: Bethanie Bourne
Picture Researcher: Liberty Newton
Reprographics: Anthony Cambray, Mike Coupe,
Stephan Davis, Ian Paulyn
Production Manager: Eliźabeth Brunwin

British Library Cataloguing-in-Publication Data
A catalogue record for this book is available from the British Library

ISBN 1-84236-773-0

Printed in China

www.mileskelly.net
info@mileskelly.net

Sharks

1000 FACTS

Anna Claybourne

Consultant: Trevor Day

MiLes KeLLy
PUBLISHING

Contents

SHARK ANATOMY

HOW SHARKS LIVE

Contents

SHARK SPECIES

SHARKS AND PEOPLE

 SHARK SCIENCE

All about sharks

- **Sharks are a type of fish**. They live and breathe underwater and are brilliant swimmers.

- **All sharks are carnivores,** which means they eat other animals. Many are fierce hunters.

- **Sharks are found** in seas and oceans and in a few rivers too.

- **There are about** 400 different species of shark.

- **A species is the name** for a particular type of shark or other living thing. Sharks of the same species can mate and have young, which also belong to that species.

- **Most sharks** have long bodies, triangle-shaped fins and lots of sharp teeth.

- **Sharks range in size** from about the size of a banana to bigger than a bus.

- **Sharks are closely related** to other fish called rays and skates. They are similar to sharks but usually have much flatter bodies.

- **Sharks have existed** for almost 400 million years.

- **Most sharks** are not dangerous. Only a few species have been known to attack humans.

▶ *A great white shark on the prowl among a shoal of fish. Many sharks hunt and eat other types of fish, as well as all kinds of sea creatures.*

Shark shapes

- **A typical shark** has a long, narrow, torpedo-shaped body, designed for moving quickly through the water.

- **All sharks,** even unusually shaped ones, have the same basic body parts: a head with eyes, nostrils and a mouth, a body, a tail and fins.

- **A body shape** designed for speed, like a shark's, is called a 'streamlined' shape. It allows water to move past it easily with very little resistance or 'drag'.

- **The tip of a shark's nose** is called the snout. Most sharks' snouts are pointed, like the tip of a bullet.

- **A shark's mouth** is usually a long way back underneath its snout.

- **Hammerhead sharks** get their name because their heads are shaped like wide, flat hammers.

- **Angel sharks** have wide, spread-out fins that look like an angel's wings.

▲ *Due to the strange shape of their heads, hammerhead sharks are probably the easiest to recognize of all sharks.*

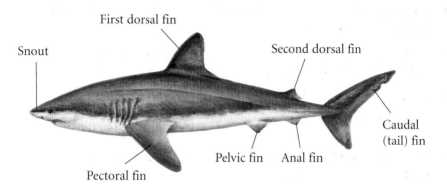

First dorsal fin

Snout

Second dorsal fin

Caudal
(tail) fin

Pelvic fin   Anal fin

Pectoral fin

▲ *Most sharks have two pectoral fins (one on each side), two pelvic fins (one on each side), two dorsal fins, an anal fin, and a caudal or tail fin.*

● **Engineers sometimes** study sharks' fins and bodies to find the best shapes for aeroplane wings or boat hulls.

● **Some large fish**, such as tuna, are shaped like sharks.

. . . **FASCINATING FACT** . . .
Some sharks can change shape. Swell sharks inflate their bodies
with water or air to make themselves bigger and rounder.

Shark sizes

- **The whale shark** is the biggest living shark. It can reach a maximum size of 18 m – as long as two buses end-to-end.

- **The biggest shark ever**, *Megalodon*, is now extinct. Scientists think it may have weighed almost twice as much a whale shark.

- **The biggest sharks** are gentle creatures that filter tiny food particles from the water.

- **The biggest hunting shark** is the great white shark.

- **A great white shark's mouth** can measure 40 cm across.

- **Most sharks are medium-sized**, measuring between 1 m and 3 m in length.

- **The smallest sharks** are the spined pygmy shark and the dwarf lanternshark. They would fit on two pages of this book.
- **The average size for a shark** is very similar to the size of a human.
- **Although some sharks** are small, most are bigger than other types of fish.
- **Sharks aren't the biggest animals** in the sea. Some whales are bigger – but they are mammals, not fish.

▼ *This is a whale shark, the biggest shark of all. It swims along with its mouth wide open in order to collect food from the water.*

Inside a shark

- **Sharks are vertebrates**, which means they have a skeleton with a backbone. Many types of animals, including all fish, reptiles, birds and mammals, are vertebrates.

- **Sharks' skeletons** are not made of bone, but of cartilage (see bendy bones).

- **If you cut a shark open**, you'd find a thick layer of muscles just under its skin. The shark uses them to move its body from side to side as it swims along.

- **A shark's vital organs** are mostly in a cavity in the middle of its body. Sharks have many of the same organs as humans and other animals, including a stomach, liver and kidneys.

- **Sharks have** extra-large livers that contain a lot of oil. As oil is lighter than water, this helps it to float.

- **A shark's stomach** is very stretchy. It can expand so that the shark can consume a large amount of food in a short space of time.

- **Just like humans**, sharks have a heart that pumps blood around their bodies.

- **Most sharks** are cold-blooded, which means their blood is the same temperature as the water around them.

- **A few sharks**, such as mako and thresher sharks, are warm-blooded – they can heat their blood up so that they are warmer than their surroundings. This helps them to swim faster and move into colder areas of the ocean to hunt.

14

▼ *Some of the main organs and other body parts of a shark's body.*

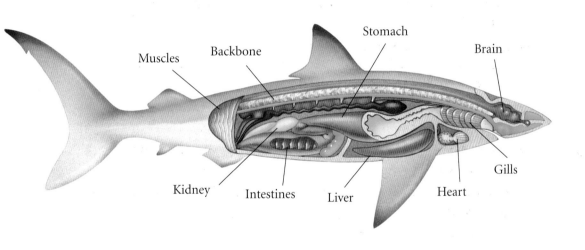

Muscles

Backbone

Stomach

Brain

Kidney

Intestines

Liver

Heart

Gills

... FASCINATING FACT ...
The insides of a shark's intestines, or guts, are spiral-shaped.
Because of this, some sharks have spiral-shaped droppings!

Bendy bones

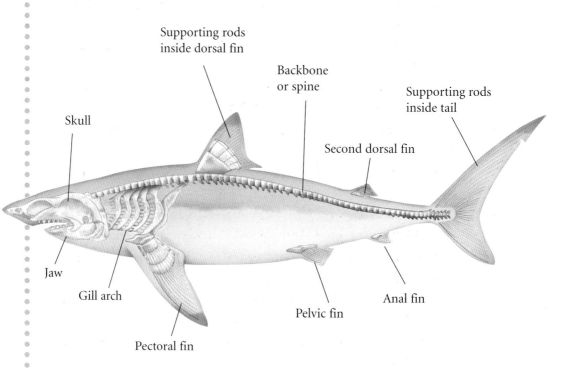

Supporting rods
inside dorsal fin

Backbone
or spine

Supporting rods
inside tail

Skull

Second dorsal fin

Jaw

Gill arch

Pectoral fin

Pelvic fin

Anal fin

▲ *The skeleton of a great white shark. The most important part is the backbone, or spine. Most other parts of the skeleton are attached to this.*

- **Cartilage is the white or pale blue,** rubbery, bendy substance that sharks' skeletons are made of.

- **A shark's bendy skeleton** gives it flexibility, helping it to twist and turn in the water.

- **Although human skeletons** are made of bone, they have a small amount of cartilage too. It can be felt in the bendy tip of the nose.

- **Cartilage can also be found** in meat. It's the tough, chewy substance that's usually called 'gristle'.

- **As well as being very flexible,** cartilage is lighter than bone, giving sharks lots of strength without making them heavy.

- **Most other fish** have bones instead of cartilage. They are called 'bony fish', while sharks, rays and skates are known as 'cartilaginous fish'.

- **Sharks' fins and tails** contain hundreds of thin rods of cartilage, which stiffen them and give them their shape.

- **A shark's spine and skull** are harder than the rest of its skeleton. They need to be stronger to hold the body together and protect the brain.

- **Sharks have simpler skeletons** than most other bony fish, with fewer ribs and other parts.

... **FASCINATING FACT** ...
Some sharks are so flexible, they can bend right around and touch their tails with their snouts.

Shark skin

- **Sharks don't have scales**, like other fish. Instead their skin is covered with tiny, hard points called denticles.

- **The word 'denticle'** means 'little tooth' – because denticles are very similar to teeth.

- **Denticles make a shark's skin** feel very rough to the touch. Some swimmers have been badly scratched just from brushing against a shark.

- **Denticles have two uses:** they protect the shark from enemies and help it to slide through the water.

- **Denticles range** from microscopic in size to about 5 mm across.

▼ *Along with its streamlined shape the denticles on a shark's skin helps it to slide smoothly through the water.*

◄ A close-up of a Greenland shark's denticles. On this part of the shark's body, the denticles are all pointing in the same direction to help water flow that way.

● **The shape of denticles** varies on different parts of a shark's body, and from one shark species to another.

● **Denticles on the side** on the side of a shark are the sharpest – ensuring fast movement through the water.

● **Sharks also release** a slimy substance from their skin, to make their bodies move through the water even faster.

● **Large sharks have very thick skin** – thicker than a human finger.

...**FASCINATING FACT**...
Shark skin is so rough that in the past it was used to make a type of sandpaper, called shagreen.

19

Tails and fins

- **A typical shark** has up to seven fins, not including its tail.

- **The big fin** on a shark's back is called the dorsal fin. It's the one that can be seen sticking out of the water in shark films and cartoons.

- **A shark's tail** is also known as its 'caudal fin'.

- **A shark's tail is made up** of two points called lobes – an upper lobe and a lower lobe.

- **There are two large pectoral** fins near the front of a shark's body, a bit like arms. The shark uses them to steer while swimming.

- **Epaulette sharks** use their pectoral fins like legs to 'crawl' along the seabed.

- **In parts of Asia**, people use sharks' fins to make a special kind of soup.

- **Thresher sharks** can be recognized by their very long upper tail lobes.

- **A whale shark's pectoral fin** can be 2 m long – that's as big as a bed!

Dorsal fin

▲ *Hammerhead sharks have very long dorsal fins.*

▶ *A shark turns, clearly showing its long pectoral fins.*

. . . FASCINATING FACT . . .
Without their fins, sharks wouldn't be able to stay
the right way up. They'd roll over in the water.

Spikes and spines

- **Many prehistoric sharks** had sharp spines in front of their dorsal fins. Scientists think these may have helped to hold the fins up.

- **Today, only a few sharks** have spines, spikes or sharp horns on their bodies. They usually use them to fight off attackers.

- **Some dogfish sharks** and horn sharks have two sharp 'fin spines' in front of their dorsal fins, which can inflict a painful wound.

- **The spined pygmy shark** is the only shark that has just one spine, not two or none.

- **Stingrays**, which are related to sharks, have poisonous stings in the middle of their tails.

- **Smaller sharks** are the most likely to have spines. That's because they are most at risk of being eaten by other animals, so they need to put off their enemies from biting them.

- **Spiny dogfish** coil themselves right around their enemies to stab them with their spines.

- **Shark spines** are made of modified, extra-large denticles.

- **Saw sharks have long**, saw-shaped snouts, edged with sharp teeth.

- **A sawfish** is a type of ray, and is closely related to sharks. Its sharp, spiky snout can grow to almost 2 m long.

▶ *Saw sharks have small, sharp spikes all the way along both sides of their long, flat snouts. They use their spiky snouts to slash at fish or to dig for prey in the seabed.*

Shark vision

▲ *When hunting, sharks such as this great white use their eyesight to help them close in accurately on their prey.*

- **Most sharks have big eyes** and good eyesight. They mainly use it to spot their prey.

- **Sharks need** to be able to see well in the dark – as there is limited light underwater.

- **Many sharks** have a shiny layer called the *tapetum lucidum* at the back of their eyes. It collects and reflects light, helping them to see, even in the gloomy darkness.

- **The *Tapetum Lucidum*** (which is Latin for 'bright carpet') makes sharks' eyes appear to glow in the dark.

- **Some sharks** have slit-shaped pupils, like a cat's.

● **Scientists think** sharks can probably see in colour, like humans.

● **Some very deepwater sharks** have small eyes and poor eyesight. That's because the deepest oceans are so dark, many animals living there rely on other senses instead.

● **Sharks have a third eye**, called a pineal eye, under the skin in their foreheads. It can't see properly like a normal eye, but it can sense daylight.

● **The shy-eye shark** gets its name because when it is caught, it covers its eyes with its tail to shield them from the light.

▲ *A close-up of a tiger shark's eye, showing a special eyelid called the nictitating membrane. This closes over the eye when the shark is about to bite, to protect it from being damaged in a struggle.*

. . .FASCINATING FACT. . .
Most sharks never close their eyes. Some have special see-through eyelids that protect their eyes without cutting out any light. Others just roll their eyes up into their head to protect them.

Sensing sounds

- **Sharks have ears**, but they're very hard to spot. Their openings are nothing more than tiny holes, just behind the shark's eyes.

- **If you think you can see** a shark's ears, you're probably looking at its spiracles (see how sharks breathe), which can look a bit like ears, but are in fact used for breathing.

- **In the sea**, sound travels in the form of vibrations rippling through the water. Sharks hear by sensing these vibrations.

- **Inside a shark's ear** is a set of looping, fluid-filled tubes called the 'labyrinth'.

- **Sharks hear** using tiny microscopic hairs inside the labyrinth. As vibrations travel through the fluid, they move the hairs, which send signals to the shark's brain.

- **Hearing is not** the shark's strongest sense, but it is its best long-distance sense. Some sharks can hear sounds from several kilometres away.

- **Sharks are best** at hearing low sounds, like the noise made by an injured animal thrashing about underwater.

- **Ears also help sharks** to keep their balance. Movements of the fluid inside their ears tell them which way up they are.

- **Some sharks have learned** to recognize the clanking sound of shark-watching cages (see shark tourism). When they hear it, sharks may travel long distances to find the cages, in the hope of being fed.

> ....FASCINATING FACT....
> Although sharks can hear sounds,
> they rarely make a noise.

26

▲ *Scientists and tourists sometimes use cages to safely get close to sharks.*

Touch and taste

- **Like us, sharks can feel** things that touch their skin. They can also feel other objects nearby, from the ripples and waves they make as water flows around them and bounces off.

- **Like humans**, sharks have millions of nerve endings all over their skin that can feel pressure, temperature and pain.

- **Sharks also have** an extra sense organ called the 'lateral line'. This is a long tube running down each side of a shark's body, under its skin.

- **As a shark swims**, ripples and currents in the water pass into the lateral line through little holes in the skin. Tiny hairs inside the lateral line sense the ripples, and send signals to the shark's brain.

Lateral line

▲ *The lateral line runs down the side of the shark's body, from its gills to its tail.*

28

- **All fish, not just sharks**, have lateral lines for sensing ripples. You might be able to see the lateral line on a fish in a fish tank or in a fishmonger's shop or supermarket.

- **Sharks also use** their sense of touch to navigate. They can 'feel' where rocks, reefs and other obstacles are, even if they can't see them.

- **Like humans**, sharks have taste buds inside their mouths.

- **As well as tasting the food they eat,** sharks can taste chemicals dissolved in the water. This helps them to find prey and avoid pollution.

- **Some sharks have** fleshy 'whiskers' on their snouts, called barbels. These can sense the location of food on the seabed.

...FASCINATING FACT...
A shark can sense a turtle, octopus or other prey from up to 20 m away.

Sensing smells

- **The sense of smell** is the most important sense for most sharks.

- **As a shark swims,** water constantly flows into the nostrils on its snout, and over the scent-detecting cells inside them.

- **Sharks can smell blood** in water, even if it's diluted to one part in ten million. That's like one drop of blood mixed into a small swimming pool.

- **A shark can smell** an injured animal up to 1 km away.

- **The biggest part** of a shark's brain is the olfactory lobe – the part used for processing smells.

- **The great white shark** has biggest olfactory lobe of all – which means it probably has the best sense of smell of any shark.

- **Swimmers have been known** to attract sharks just by having a tiny scratch on their skin.

- **Sharks use their nostrils** for smelling, not breathing.

- **A shark homes in on a scent** by zig-zagging its snout from side to side. It moves towards the side where the smell is strongest.

> ...FASCINATING FACT...
> In one experiment, a scientist plugged one of
> a shark's nostrils. It swam around in a circle!

▶ *A great white shark hunting, trying to detect traces of blood from injured fish or other animals. The water flows into the nostrils at the front of its snout as it swims along.*

The sixth sense

▼ *The ampullae of Lorenzini scattered across a shark's snout can be seen clearly here. Each ampulla looks like a tiny hole or pit. Under the surface of the skin, it opens out into a wider bottle shape, containing a jelly that collects electrical signals.*

- **A shark has six senses**. Besides having vision, hearing, touch, taste and smell, sharks can also sense the small amounts of electricity given off by other animals.

- **To detect electricity**, a shark has tiny holes in the skin around its head and snout. They're called the 'ampullae of Lorenzini'.

- **Ampullae** are a type of Roman bottle. The ampullae of Lorenzini get their name because of their narrow-necked bottle shape.

- **Each ampulla** contains a jelly-like substance that collects electric signals.

- **All animals** give off tiny amounts of electricity when their muscles move. Electricity doesn't travel well through air, but it travels well through water.

- **A shark's ampullae of Lorenzini** can sense animals within a range of about one metre.

- **Some sharks** use their electrical sense to find prey that's buried in the seabed.

- **A fierce hunting shark**, such as a tiger or hammerhead, has up to 1500 ampullae of Lorenzini.

- **Stefano Lorenzini** was an Italian anatomist (body scientist). He studied the ampullae of Lorenzini, and gave them their name, in 1678.

> ....FASCINATING FACT....
> Some other animals can detect electricity
> too – including the duck-billed platypus.

33

Smart sharks

- **Most sharks have big brains** for their body size and are probably cleverer than many bony fish.

- **Almost all** of a shark's brain is used for processing information from the senses.

- **The brain parts** used for learning and thinking are quite small in sharks.

- **In relation to their body size**, hammerhead sharks have the biggest brains.

- **In captivity**, some sharks have learned to do simple tasks in exchange for a reward.

- **Experiments with lemon sharks** show they can tell between different shapes and colours.

- **Some sharks** are brighter than others. Fast hunters such as great whites are the most intelligent. Slow-moving bottom-feeders like carpet sharks are less smart.

- **Scientists used to think** all sharks had little intelligence. They have only recently started to learn about how their brains work.

- **Sharks can be trained** to fetch rubber rings, just like a dog fetching a stick.

> ...**FASCINATING FACT**...
> Sharks' brains aren't round like ours –
> they are long and narrow .

▼ *A scalloped hammerhead, one of the smartest sharks. Hammerhead sharks are fast, fierce hunters. They also spend time in groups and scientists think they have simple social systems.*

How sharks breathe

◀ *A silky shark. All five gill slits on the side of the shark's throat can be clearly seen.*

- **Like most animals**, sharks need to take in oxygen to make their bodies work.

- **Like other fish**, sharks breathe underwater using gills in their throats.

- **Most sharks have five pairs of gills**. Each gill is made up of a set of feathery, hair-like filaments full of blood vessels.

- **Many sharks** have extra breathing holes called spiracles, just behind their eyes, that take in water for the shark to breathe.

- **As a shark swims**, water flows into its mouth or spiracles, and past the gills. They take oxygen out of the water and carry it into the shark's bloodstream.

- **The water flows out again** through the gill slits – the lines you can see on the sides of a shark's neck.

- **Sharks don't have lungs** – their gills do the same job that lungs do in humans.

- **Some fast sharks**, such as mako sharks, have to keep swimming in order to keep breathing. If they stop, water stops flowing past their gills and they suffocate.

- **Slow-moving sharks** such as the Port Jackson shark can pump water across their gills, so they can stop for a rest and still keep breathing.

> **. . . FASCINATING FACT . . .**
> Sea water contains just one percent oxygen gas –
> much less than air, which is 21 percent oxygen.

37

How sharks swim

▶ *White-tip reef sharks often stop swimming to rest on the seabed. As they are heavier than water, they have to start swimming again if they want to move off the seabed.*

- **A shark's main swimming organ** is its tail. The shark thrashes it from side to side to push itself through the water.

- **Sharks use their pectoral** and pelvic fins to help them steer and swim upwards and downwards.

- **The fastest shark** is the shortfin mako shark, which has been recorded swimming at over 30 km/hour.

- **Most sharks have** an everyday cruising speed of around 8km/hour.

- **Sharks normally swim** with a relaxed, regular rhythm. They don't dart around like most bony fish do.

> ...FASCINATING FACT...
> If sharks don't keep swimming, they
> gradually sink onto the seabed.

- **Other bony fish** have a swim bladder – a gas-filled organ that keeps them afloat. But sharks don't have swim bladders, so they are slightly heavier than water.

- **Many sharks swim** in a figure-of-eight pattern when they are annoyed.

- **Thanks to their streamlined shape**, sharks can swim very quietly and sneak up on their prey.

- **Some sharks swallow air** to help them to float better.

▼ *A shark's torpedo-shaped body makes it a very fast swimmer.*

Shark teeth

- **A hunting shark**, such as a great white or a tiger shark, has several rows of teeth.

- **A shark's gums** are like a conveyor belt. The rows of teeth constantly move slowly forwards. Gradually the front row wears out, and a new row replaces them.

- **Only the two front rows of teeth** are used for biting. The rest are just lining up to replace them.

▼ *A great white shark stretches its mouth wide open, revealing its sharp, triangle-shaped teeth.*

40

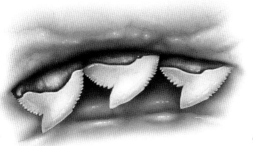

◀ *A tiger shark's teeth, have very sharp, serrated edges, like a sharp knife. This helps the teeth to cut through meat.*

● **In a lifetime**, some sharks will get through 30,000 teeth altogether.

● **You can sometimes find** sharks' old, used teeth washed up on beaches.

● **Shark's teeth** really are as sharp as razors. Each tooth has serrated edges, with tiny, sharp points on them, like a saw, for cutting through meat.

● **The biggest shark teeth** belong to the great white shark. They can grow to over 6 cm long.

● **Some sharks**, such as smooth-houndsharks, don't have sharp biting teeth. Instead they have hard, flat plates in their mouths for grinding up crabs and shellfish.

● **The sand tiger shark** has the deadliest-looking teeth – but they are only used for catching small fish.

. . . FASCINATING FACT . . .
A typical shark has several hundred
teeth at any one time.

41

What sharks eat

- **Most sharks eat** many different kinds of animals.

- **Big, fast hunting sharks**, such as great whites and bull sharks, feed on large fish (including other sharks), as well as seals, turtles, octopuses, squid, seabirds and other sea creatures.

- **Many smaller sharks**, such as dogfish sharks, hunt smaller fish, octopuses and squid.

- **Slow-moving sharks**, such as nurse sharks, angel sharks and carpet sharks, crunch up crabs, shrimps and shellfish that they find on the seabed.

- **Filter-feeders** are sharks that feed on plankton – tiny floating animals and plants – which they filter out of the water.

- **There are hardly any** animal species in the sea that aren't part of the diet of one shark or another.

- **Tiger sharks** are well-known for eating anything they can find, including objects that aren't food, such as tin cans.

- **After being eaten**, food stays in a shark's stomach for up to three days.

- **Most sharks don't eat every day.** Some big hunters can go without food for months.

> ...FASCINATING FACT...
> Sharks generally prefer the taste of fish,
> seals and turtles to the taste of humans.

▲ *Hammerhead sharks prey on other sharks, rays, bony fish, crabs and lobsters, octopuses and squid.*

How sharks hunt

- **Most sharks are nocturnal** – which means they hunt at night – or crepuscular – which means they hunt at dusk.

- **Before attacking**, some sharks 'bump' their prey with their snouts, probably to see if it's something edible and tasty.

- **When about to bite**, a shark raises its snout and thrusts its jaws forward, so that its teeth stick out to grab the prey.

- **Some sharks shake their prey** from side to side to rip it apart.

- **Sharks don't usually chew** – they tear their prey into chunks or just swallow it whole.

- **Sharks can attack** animals much bigger than themselves. For example, great whites have been known to bite chunks out of whales.

- **Sometimes**, lots of sharks are attracted to a source of food, and they all jostle to eat it at the same time. This is known as a 'feeding frenzy'.

- **Most hunting sharks** prefer prey that's weak or helpless, because it's easier to catch. That's why sharks are good at smelling blood – it tells them when an animal is injured.

- **Many sharks give their prey** a fatal bite, then leave it to bleed to death. They then return to feed on the body.

> **...FASCINATING FACT...**
> Sharks have very strong jaws. They can bite other animals in half – even those with tough shell, such as turtles.

▼ *This great white shark is about to take a bite out of a piece of meat dangled from a boat. Although it's not hunting, you can see how it lifts its snout up high and thrusts its teeth forward to attack.*

Filter-feeding

- **The biggest sharks of all** – whale sharks, basking sharks and megamouths – eat the smallest prey – plankton. These sharks are the filter-feeders.

- **Plankton** is made up of small sea creatures such as shrimps, baby crabs and octopuses, and tiny free-floating plants. It drifts along with the currents.

- **Filter-feeding sharks** have 'gill rakers' – special comblike bristles in their throats that sieve plankton out of the water.

- **Gill rakers** are coated in sticky mucus to help plankton to stick to them.

- **Filter-feeding sharks** swallow the plankton they have collected, while the water they have sieved escapes from their gills.

- **Filter-feeders** have massive mouths so they can suck in as much water as possible.

- **To collect a kilogram of plankton**, a shark has to filter one million litres of water – enough to fill nearly half an olympic-sized swimming pool.

- **In one hour**, a whale shark filters around 2 million litres of water, and collects 2 kg of food.

- **Whale sharks** sometimes suck in shoals of little fish, such as sardines, that are also busy feeding on plankton.

- **Some other big sea creatures** – such as the blue whale, the world's biggest animal – are also filter-feeders.

▼ *Whale sharks are filter-feeders. Although they are huge, they feed on some of the tiniest animals in the sea – plankton.*

Plankton —

47

Scavenging

- **Scavenging means feeding** on other hunters' leftovers, dying animals or the bodies of animals that have already died.

- **Almost all sharks** will scavenge if they can't find other food.

- **Some sharks**, such as the Greenland shark and the smooth dogfish, get a lot of their food by scavenging.

...FASCINATING FACT...
In Australia in 1935, a tiger shark vomited up a human arm. The shark
had not killed anyone but had scavenged the arm after a murder victim
had been cut up with a knife and thrown into the sea.

- **In the deepest parts of the ocean**, sharks and other animals often feed on the bodies of dead sea creatures that sink down from higher levels.

- **Sharks are much more likely** to eat people who have already drowned than they are to attack living people.

- **Sharks scavenge** humans' food too – especially waste food that's thrown overboard from ships.

- **Sharks sometimes eat fish** caught in fishing boats' nets before they can be pulled to the surface.

- **Although they are thought of** as the ultimate killers, great white sharks love to scavenge – especially on the bodies of dead whales.

- **Scavenging** is kind of natural recycling. It keeps the oceans clean, and makes sure leftovers and dead animals are rapidly recycled rather than left to slowly decompose.

◀ *A great white shark attacking a chunk of meat attached to a float and line. Sharkwatchers make use of the shark's scavenging behaviour to draw fish close to the boat.*

Lighting up

- **Some sharks** can glow in the dark.

- **When animals give** off light, it's known as bioluminescence, which means 'living light'.

- **Glowing sharks** are often found in the deepest oceans where it is particularly dark.

- **Some deep-sea glowing sharks**, such as dwarf dogfish and velvet belly shark, may use their lights to light up their surroundings and help them see their prey.

- **Lanternsharks** have glowing dots around and inside their mouths. This may attract small fish and lure them into the shark's mouth.

- **Some sharks that live** at medium depths have glowing undersides. This makes them hard to see from below, as their light bellies match the light coming down from the sea surface.

- **Sharks may use** bioluminescence to communicate. For example, green dogfish sharks feed in groups. Their light patterns may help them to find each other.

- **Glowing lights** may also have another use – helping sharks to find a mate of their own species in the darkness of the deep ocean.

- **Bioluminescence is made** in tiny organs in the skin called 'photophores'. In a photophore, two chemicals are combined, creating a chemical reaction that gives off light.

- **Some other animals** have bioluminescence too. They include deep sea fish such as the anglerfish, as well as fireflies and some types of worms.

▲ *Lanternsharks get their name from the glowing lights on their bodies. Their 'glow' comes from tiny light-emitting organs called photophores.*

51

Staying safe

▲ *When great white sharks feel threatened, they open their mouths wide to show off their sharp teeth.*

- **Smaller sharks make a tasty snack** for other animals. These sharks need to defend themselves against hungry predators such as killer whales, dolphins and porpoises.

- **The biggest sharks** are rarely eaten by other sea creatures, but they can still be hunted by humans.

- **Sharks are good at hiding.** They slip in between rocks, or into caves in coral reefs, to escape from their enemies.

- **When in danger**, some sharks start swimming in a jerky, random manner to confuse their attacker.

- **Thresher sharks** can use their extra-long tails for fighting off predators, as well as for attacking their own prey.

- **Swell sharks can inflate** their bodies while in a crack between rocks. This jams the shark into the crack so that it can't be pulled out by a predator.

- **Sharks' tough, thick skin** acts like armour, making it harder for predators to bite them.

- **Sharks with spines**, such as horn sharks, can often put a predator off by giving it a sharp stab.

- **Most sharks are scared of humans.** If they hear divers nearby, they usually swim away at once.

> ...FASCINATING FACT...
> As another way to put off attackers, sharks can turn their stomachs inside out and vomit up their latest meal. Some predators eat the vomit instead of the shark.

Sharks in disguise

- **Many sharks** are good at disguising themselves to look like their surroundings. This is called camouflage.

- **Camouflage** is a good way to hide from enemies, but it can also be used to help sharks sneak up on their prey without being seen.

- **Many small sharks**, such as zebra sharks, epaulette sharks and wobbegongs, have brown or grey spots, blotches and patterns to help them blend in with coral and seaweed.

- **Sharks are often darker** on their top half, and paler on their bottom half. This is called countershading.

- **How does countershading work**? Viewed from below, the shark blends in with the brightly-lit sea surface and sky. Seen from above, it blends in with the murky depths.

- **Some wobbegong sharks** have barbels that look like seaweed around their mouths. The fake seaweed tricks fish to come close enough for the wobbegong to catch.

- **Angel sharks have very flat**, smooth bodies. When they lie on the sandy seabed, they become almost invisible.

- **The shovelnose shark** or guitarfish (really a type of ray) disguises itself by burying itself under the seabed, with only its eyes sticking out.

- **The cookie-cutter shark** uses patches of bioluminescent light on its skin to attract hunting fish, seals, or whales to come closer – then the cookie-cutter takes a bite out of them.

- **When leopard sharks** are young, they have leopard-like spots to help them hide. As they get older and bigger, they don't need so much protection, and the spots fade.

▼ *A silvertip shark demonstrates the countershading that many sharks have: pale skin on the underside, and darker skin above.*

Loners and groups

- **Many sharks**, such as whale sharks and bull sharks, are solitary. That means they like to live, hunt and travel alone.

- **Sharks don't live in families**. They meet up to mate, but a mating pair do not live together. Their young do not live with them either.

- **Some sharks form groups** with other members of their species. White-tip reef sharks, for example, often rest together in small groups of about ten individuals.

- **Sharks probably gather in groups** because there's safety in numbers. Several sharks together are less likely to be attacked than a single shark.

- **Hammerhead sharks** prefer to live in groups. They travel in huge shoals of hundreds of sharks.

- **Spending time in a group** may help sharks to meet a mate.

- **Some species, such as lemon sharks**, form single-sex groups of just males or just females. Scientists are not sure why.

  - **Porbeagle sharks** have been seen playing together in groups of about 20.

    - **Although great white sharks** are usually solitary, scientists have found that they sometimes make companions and hunt in pairs.

▲ *Several hammerhead sharks swimming together in a group. Hammerheads like to spend time in large groups, but many species of sharks prefer to live alone.*

...FASCINATING FACT...
Groups of nurse sharks sometimes relax
by lying in a heap on the seabed.

Communication

- **Animals don't have complicated languages** like humans do – but they can still communicate in different ways.

- **When they are close together**, sharks can 'talk' using body language. They make different shapes and postures, just as humans show their feelings by making faces.

- **For example**, when a shark is annoyed or frightened, it arches its back, raises its snout, and points its pectoral fins down.

- **Sharks also release special scents** called pheromones to send messages to other sharks. These can indicate if a shark is looking for a mate or feeling agitated.

- **Many other animals** use pheromones too, including moths, bees, pigs, deer, and humans.

- **When sharks live in a group**, the biggest, strongest ones usually become the leaders. They sometimes have small fights with the other sharks to show their dominance.

- **Bioluminescence** (lighting up) helps some sharks to communicate. It can help a shark recognize another shark of the same species in the dark (see lighting up).

- **Sharks may also be able to** recognize each other by the ripples and splashes their bodies make as they swim, which other sharks can feel (see touch and taste).

- **A few shark species** have been heard making sounds. For example, swell sharks sometimes make a barking noise. But experts are not yet sure if it's a way of 'talking'.

...FASCINATING FACT...
One shark kept in captivity was able to detect the minute
electrical current generated by corroding metal near its tank,
and kept butting the tank at that point.

▼ *This shark is displaying an aggressive posture. Its upward-pointed snout, arched back and downward-pointed fins mean it's in a bad mood and ready to attack.*

Meeting and mating

◀ *Male white-tip reef sharks sometimes spend time resting in shallow water during the day. If they smell a pheromone scent from a female telling them she's looking for a mate, they will try to find her.*

- **Like most animals**, sharks have to mate in order to reproduce.

- **Mating happens** when a male and a female of the same species meet up, and the male gives the female some cells from his body. This allows her to make new young inside her body.

- **Nurse sharks**, blue sharks and many other species have special mating areas in shallow parts of the sea.

- **In other species**, such as white-tip reef sharks, the females release pheromones to help the males find them.

- **Male sharks sometimes bite** female sharks to show they want to mate with them.

- **Female sharks** often have thicker skin than males so that being bitten during courtship doesn't harm them.

- **When sharks mate**, the male uses two body parts called claspers to deliver cells into an opening in the female's body, called the cloaca.

- **Sharks often wind their bodies** around each other when they are mating.

- **Sharks don't mate very often.** In most species, they only reproduce only once every two years.

> ...FASCINATING FACT...
> The ancient Greek scientist and writer Aristotle studied and wrote about how sharks mate over 2300 years ago.

Shark eggs

- **Many sharks have young** by laying eggs, as most bony fish do. Sharks that do this are called 'oviparous' sharks.

- **Bullhead**, dogfish, horn, zebra and swell sharks are all oviparous sharks.

- **A typical shark** lays between 10 and 20 eggs at a time.

- **A mother shark** doesn't guard her eggs. She lays them in a safe place, such as between two rocks or under a clump of seaweed, then leaves them to hatch.

- **Sharks' eggs** are enclosed in protective egg cases. The egg cases come in many shapes, including tubes, spirals and pillow shapes.

- **When the female** first lays her eggs, their cases are soft, but when they come in contact with the seawater, they get harder.

- **Like a chicken's egg**, a shark egg contains a yolk that feeds the baby as it grows bigger.

- **Inside the egg**, a shark baby grows for between six and ten months before hatching.

- **You can sometimes find empty** shark eggcases washed up on beaches. They're known as 'mermaid's purses'.

▶ *A fully-formed Port Jackson shark emerges from its spiral-shaped egg case.*

▲ *A mother Port Jackson shark laying an egg. After laying, female Port Jackson sharks pick up their egg cases in their mouths and wedge them into safe place, such as between two rocks.*

Shark young

- **Not all sharks lay eggs**. Some give birth to live young instead. They're called 'viviparous' or 'ovoviviparous' sharks.

- **In ovoviviparous sharks**, such as basking sharks, the young grow inside eggs, but hatch while they are still inside the mother's body, before being born.

- **In viviparous sharks**, such as hammerheads, there are no eggs. The babies grow inside the mother's body from the start.

- **Young sharks** are called pups.

- **When a shark pup** is born alive, it usually slips out of its mother's body tail-first.

- **Most shark pups** look like smaller versions of their parents, but with a narrower body shape and stronger colours.

- **Some species**, such as sand tiger sharks, have just two pups in a litter.

- **Whale sharks are thought** to be able to give birth to up to 300 pups at a time.

- **Shark parents** don't look after their babies. Once a pup is born, or hatches from its egg, it has to look after itself.

> ...FASCINATING FACT...
> In sand tiger sharks and several other species, the biggest, strongest pups eat the others while they are still inside their mother's body.

▼ *Tiger shark pups are usually born at the end of spring or the beginning of summer. There can be between 10 and 80 pups in a litter. Like all young sharks, tiger shark pups have to look after themselves and start hunting for food at once.*

Growing up

- **Sharks grow slowly.** It can take a pup up to 20 years to grow into an adult.

- **Blue sharks** are among the fastest growers. A blue shark pup grows about 30 cm longer every year, changing from a 50-cm long pup to an adult up to 4 m long.

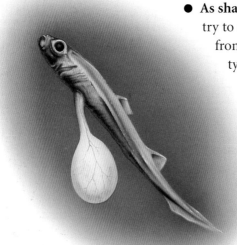

- **As shark pups are small**, predators often try to eat them. The biggest danger comes from other adult sharks that prey on any type of smaller fish. Sometimes, pups even get eaten by adults of their own species.

- **For every ten shark pups** born, only one or two will survive to be adults.

- **Many types of shark pups** live in 'nursery areas' – shallow parts of the sea close to the shore, where there are plenty of hiding places to shelter in and smaller sea creatures to feed on.

▲ *As a baby shark develops, it feeds on the yolk from its egg. This is a lanternshark pup with its yolk.*

> ....FASCINATING FACT....
> Even when they reach adulthood, sharks don't
> stop growing. They just grow more slowly.

- **Sharks are born** with a full set of teeth (see shark teeth), so they can start hunting for their own food straight away. Unlike the young of birds, humans, dogs and cats, shark pups are never fed by their parents.

- **Young sharks** eat things such as small fish, shrimps and baby octopuses. As sharks grow bigger, they hunt bigger prey.

- **A typical shark** lives for around 25 to 30 years, although some species, including whale sharks and dogfish sharks, may live for 100 years or more.

- **When a shark dies**, scientists can tell how old it is by counting growth rings in its spine – like the rings inside tree trunks.

▼ Once a large shark, such as this great white, reaches adulthood, it is several metres long, and there are few other animals in the sea that can harm it.

- **There are several types** of sea creatures that like to hang around sharks. They include some fish species, and many parasites that feed on a shark's skin, blood or insides.

- **Small crablike creatures** called copepods attach themselves to a shark's eyes, gills, snout or fins. They nibble the shark's skin or suck its blood.

- **Sea leeches** bite sharks on their undersides and suck their blood.

- **Barnacles are tiny sea creatures** with shells. They fix themselves to rocks, boats, and large animals such as whales and sharks.

- **Whale sharks** sometimes try to get rid of skin parasites by rubbing themselves against boats.

- **Inside their bodies**, many sharks have parasites such as tapeworms. They live in a shark's gut and feed on its food.

- **Pilot fish swim alongside sharks** to hitch a ride on the shark's slipstream – the currents it makes in the water.

- **Sometimes a shark and another species** can help each other. This kind of relationship between two animals is called 'symbiosis'.

- **Sharks open their mouths** to let tiny cleaner wrasse fish nibble lice and dead skin from between their teeth. As the wrasse are helping the sharks, they don't get eaten.

- **Remoras or 'shark suckers'** are fish that attach themselves to sharks using suction pads on their heads. They hitch a ride on the shark's body and feed on scraps of food left over by the shark.

◀ *A silvertip shark with a much smaller fish swimming along in its slipstream.*

Where sharks live

- **Sharks are found** in seas and oceans all around the world.

- **Sharks are almost all marine fish** – which means they live in the salty sea rather than in fresh water.

- **Just a few shark species** such as bull sharks and Ganges sharks can survive in fresh water, and swim out of the sea into rivers and lakes.

- **Sharks are most common** around coasts. Many species like to live in shallow sandy bays, near coral reefs, or in the medium-deep water a few miles from the shore.

- **Coral reefs and seaweed forests** are an especially good home for young sharks. They provide them with food and hiding places.

- **Sharks that live out in the open ocean**, such as blue sharks, are known as pelagic sharks.

- **Many types of sharks**, such as wobbegongs, spend most of their time on the ocean floor. They're called benthic sharks.

- **Many sharks prefer warm waters**, such as those around Africa, Australia, Japan, and North and South America – but a few, such as the Greenland shark, live in cold water around the Arctic.

- **Sharks are hardly ever found** in the Southern Ocean around Antarctica – probably because it's too cold for them there.

> **...FASCINATING FACT...**
> Epaulette sharks are often found in rock pools. They can move
> from one pool to another across dry land, by dragging
> themselves with their strong pectoral fins.

▼ *A scalloped hammerhead shark cruises across a coral reef – an underwater structure built by tiny creatures called coral polyps.*

Sharks at home

- **Most sharks don't have a fixed home**. They just swim around anywhere they like, looking for food or seeking a mate.

- **Sharks don't build nests**, dig burrows, or make any other kind of shelter.

- **A territory is an area** that a wild animal marks out for itself and guards against rivals.

- **Big cats, bears** and many other animals are territorial (have territories), but scientists are still trying to find out how territorial sharks are.

- **Some shark species**, such as the grey reef shark, seem to have a territory that they patrol and guard.

- **White-tip reef sharks** stay in the same area for several months or years, although they don't defend it like a true territory.

- **Some sharks, such as horn sharks**, pick a special nursery area to lay their eggs in. Females may guard their nesting area against other females.

- **Some shark species,** such as nurse sharks, use underwater sea caves as a place to rest during the day.

- **Some sharks** have special preferences about where they live. For example, the Galapagos shark is only found around groups of small oceanic islands.

> ...FASCINATING FACT...
> The Portuguese shark has been found in depths
> of 2640 m – deeper than any other shark.

▲ *A nurse shark rests quietly in a cave in a coral reef. Although sharks don't build their own homes like some other animals, some do use caves as hiding places.*

Long-distance travel

- **Many types of sharks** travel long distances in the course of their lives.
- **As all the world's seas and oceans** are connected, it's easy for sharks to cover huge distances.
- **Dogfish sharks** that are tagged and released back into the sea can be located over 8000 km away from where they were first caught.
- **Migrating** means moving around, usually from season to season, according to a regular pattern.
- **Blue sharks** make the longest migrations. They follow the Gulf Stream current across the Atlantic from the Caribbean Sea to Europe, then swim south along the African coast, then cross the Atlantic again to return to the Caribbean.
- **A blue shark** can cover a distance of more than 6000 km in one year.
- **Sharks sometimes migrate** in order to mate in one part of the sea, then move far away to another area to lay their eggs somewhere safer.
- **Another reason for sharks** to migrate is to follow shoals of fish as they move around the oceans, in order to feed on them.
- **Scientists think sharks** may use their ampullae of Lorenzini to detect the Earth's magnetic field, helping them to navigate over long distances.
- **Many sharks**, like spined pygmy sharks, spend the daytime in deep water, but swim up to the surface at night. This is called vertical migration.

◄ *This dogfish shark has been tagged by scientists so that they can keep track of how far it travels.*

Types of sharks

- **Scientists divide the 400 species**, of sharks into eight large groups, called orders, and around 30 smaller groups, or families.

- **Arranging sharks into groups**, or 'classifying' them, helps scientists to study them and identify them.

- **Scientists often disagree** about how to classify sharks. Different shark experts have invented several different ways of grouping them.

- **Shark orders and families** have long scientific names. For example, goblin sharks belong to the *Mitsukurinidae* family, in the order *Lamniformes*.

- **Some shark groups** have common names too. The *Lamniformes*, for example, are also known as mackerel sharks.

- **Like all animals**, each shark species also has its own scientific name, which is written in Latin. For example, the great white shark is *Carcharodon carcharias*.

- **Scientists decide what group** a shark belongs to by looking at things like its body shape, markings and behaviour.

- **Sometimes, very different-looking sharks** can belong to the same group. Huge whale sharks and small, slender epaulette sharks, for example, are both in the same order.

- **Some sharks** have several different names. For example, the sand tiger shark can also be called the sand shark, the grey nurse shark, or the ragged-tooth shark.

- **There may still be** unknown types of sharks that scientists have not yet discovered.

▼ *This is a silky shark. It belongs to the family* Carcharhinidae – *also called requiem sharks – in the order* Carcharhiniformes, *and its Latin name is* Carcharhinus falciformis.

Great white sharks

▼ A great white shark about to bite, fits in with most people's idea of a dangerous shark.

- **The most famous** and feared of all sharks is the great white.

- **Belonging to** the mackerel shark group, great white sharks are fast, fierce hunters.

- **A typical great white shark** is around 4 to 5 m long – slightly longer than a car.

- **The biggest great whites** on record were over 7 m long.

- **Great white sharks** are usually found in medium-warm waters such as those around North America, Australia and Japan.

- **Great whites** do sometimes attack humans, but their favourite foods are fish, seals and sealions.

- **Great white sharks** are not white all over. They are grey on top, with a pale grey or creamy-white underside.

- **Sea fishermen report** that great whites sometimes stick their heads out of the water, or even leap high into the air.

- **Great white sharks** can't be kept in captivity. If they are caught and put into a tank or aquarium, they only live for a few days.

...FASCINATING FACT...
Little is actually known about great white sharks. Scientists do not know exactly how they reproduce, where they migrate to or how long they live.

Mako sharks

- **Swift and fierce** makos are strong, muscular hunting sharks that can swim at great speed.

- **Makos are closely related** to great white sharks and live and hunt in a similar way.

- **Makos have long**, streamlined bodies with very pointed snouts, and grow up to 4 m long.

- **Makos are known for their vivid colours**. They are dark purplish-blue on top and silvery-white underneath. They have been described as the most beautiful of all sharks.

- **There are two species of mako** – the shortfin and the longfin. The longfin has longer pectoral fins.

- **The name 'mako'** comes from the Maori name for the shark, mako-mako – which means 'man-eater'. Makos are common around New Zealand, the home of the Maori people. They are also found in oceans all around the world.

- **Makos sometimes attack humans** but they usually eat fish.

- **Mako sharks' teeth** are very narrow and pointed to help them grab slippery fish in their jaws.

- **People often fish** for makos as a sport and they are also caught to use as food.

- **Makos are** also known as bonito sharks or blue pointers.

▶ *The shortfin mako is the faster of the two species of mako shark.*

Shark species

Thresher sharks

- **There are three species of threshers** – the common, the pelagic, and the bigeye thresher.

- **Thresher sharks** are easily recognized by their extremely long tails. The upper lobe, or part, of a thresher's tail can be up to 50 percent of the shark's whole body length

- **Including the tail,** threshers can grow up to 6 m long.

▼ *Thresher sharks use their enormous tails by sweeping them from side to side. Because the tail is so long, its sweeping or 'threshing' movements can hit dozens of fish at once.*

- **Threshers use their amazing tails** to round up shoals of small fish such as sardines or herrings. Then they stun the fish by beating (or 'threshing') them with their tails, before eating them.

- **Although threshers are big**, their mouths are small so they only eat small prey.

- **Threshers hardly ever attack humans**. But they have been known to injure fishermen by hitting them with their tails.

- **Common threshers** are the best-known and are often seen near the shore.

- **Pelagic threshers** get their name because they prefer to stay in the pelagic zone – the open sea, away from the shore.

- **Bigeye threshers** often live deep down in the sea. Their eyes are up to 10 cm across (see shark records).

...FASCINATING FACT...
Thresher sharks have a reputation for being very cunning. Because of this, the ancient Greeks and Romans called them 'fox sharks'.

Sand tiger sharks

- **A typical sand tiger shark** is around 3.2 m long.

- **Sand tiger sharks** are not a type of tiger shark, and aren't closely related to tiger sharks. They belong to a different order, and are more closely related to makos and great whites.

- **Sand tiger sharks** don't have stripes – they have brownish spots instead.

- **The name** sand tiger shark is given because they like to swim over the sandy seabed near the shore, and because of their large teeth.

- **Sharks often circle** around their prey before closing in for the kill.

- **Sand tigers** are not very dangerous to humans.

- **The diet** of sand tiger sharks is mainly fish and sometimes they kill and eat bigger animals such as sealions.

- **When hunting,** sand tiger sharks sometimes work in groups. They may surround a shoal of fish and feed on them all together, in a 'feeding frenzy'.

- **Sand tigers are popular** in zoos and aquariums, as they look frightening and exciting and survive well in captivity.

...FASCINATING FACT...
Sand tiger sharks have been known to approach divers who are spear-fishing, and grab the fish off their spears.

▲ *A sand tiger shark in the Coex Aquarium in South Korea eating another shark. This sand tiger caused problems at the aquarium by eating several of its tank-mates.*

Porbeagle sharks

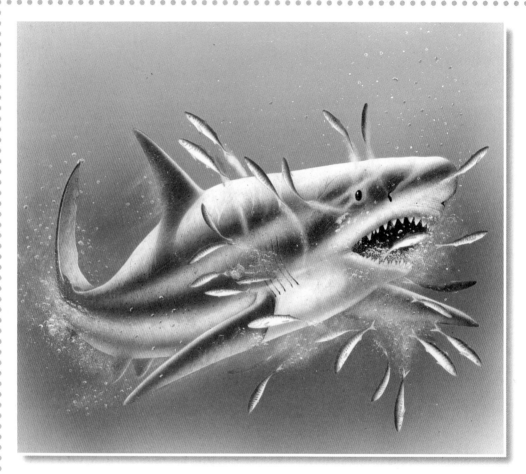

▲ *A porbeagle shark chasing mackerel, its favourite food. Porbeagles can travel long distances following shoals of mackerel around the ocean.*

- **To help porbeagle sharks** swim faster they have a second keel, or ridge, on their tails. This makes them powerful swimmers.

- **Like great white sharks,** porbeagles are grey on top and white underneath. You can tell the difference because porbeagles also have a white mark on the dorsal fin.

- **Porbeagle sharks** grow up to 3 m long.

- **Cooler seas**, such as the north and south Atlantic Ocean, are the preferred habitat of porbeagle sharks.

- **Porbeagles can make their bodies warmer** than their surroundings. This helps them to stay warm in their chilly habitat.

- **Porbeagle sharks** used to be known as mackerel sharks.

- **The diet of porbeagles is mostly fish and squid.** They sometimes chase shoals of mackerel long distances to feed on them.

- **Porbeagles are aggressive** and can attack people. However, these are very rare, because people don't usually swim in cold water.

- **Porbeagle sharks** are among the few fish that are known to play. They roll over and over at the sea surface, wrap themselves in seaweed, and throw objects around.

- **The name 'porbeagle'** is thought to come from a combination of porpoise (which the porbeagle resembles) and beagle, a dog known for its determination and toughness.

Basking sharks

- **Unlike its cousins**, great whites and makos, the basking shark is a gentle giant, not a fierce hunter.

- **The basking shark** is the second-biggest shark in the world, after the whale shark. It grows up to 9 m long – as long as five people lying end-to-end.

- **Basking sharks** are filter-feeders, and eat by sieving tiny animals, known as plankton, out of the water as they swim along.

- **Basking sharks** are not interested in eating humans – as they don't have big teeth for biting or chewing.

▲ *Basking sharks often appear to have hexagonal or ripple patterns on their backs. These are caused by sunlight shining through the waves onto the shark, which often swims near the sea surface.*

- **Basking sharks get their name** because they appear to 'bask', or lie in the sun, close to the surface of the sea. In fact, when they do this they are probably feeding.

◀ Krill are like tiny prawns. They are just one of the many small sea animals that make up plankton.

- **Basking sharks** sometimes leap right out of the water, then flop back down with a huge splash. This can be dangerous to humans if the shark lands on a boat.

- **Other names** for baskings sharks have been bone sharks, elephant sharks, bigmouth sharks, or sunfish – because people used to think basking sharks enjoyed lying in the sun.

- **Occasionally** basking sharks have been seen swimming in large groups of 50 or more.

- **People used to catch basking sharks** and collect the oil from their livers to use as lamp fuel. Because basking sharks are so big, one basking shark liver could provide a huge amount of lamp oil.

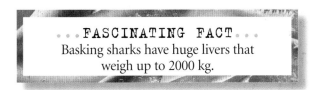

...**FASCINATING FACT**...
Basking sharks have huge livers that
weigh up to 2000 kg.

89

Goblin sharks

▲ *Even when their jaws are not thrust out, goblin sharks are instantly recognizable by their flat, sharp-edged snouts and bubblegum-pink colour.*

- **With incredibly long**, flattened, pointed snouts goblin sharks look very strange. They can stick their jaws right out of their heads.

- **The goblin shark's long snout** looks like a weapon – but in fact, scientists think it probably helps the shark find prey using its sense of electrical detection (see the sixth sense).

- **Goblin sharks have pale pink skin** which is much softer and flabbier than the skin of most sharks.

- **When its jaws are not pushed forward,** the goblin shark looks similar to other sharks.

- **When it is about to catch prey,** a goblin shark thrusts its jaws out so far, they look like a second snout.

- **Goblin sharks feed on fish,** squid, and crustaceans such as crabs and lobsters.

- **A goblin shark has sharp teeth** at the front of its mouth for grabbing prey, and smaller teeth at the back of its mouth for crunching and chewing.

- **Most goblin sharks** are between 1 m to 2 m long, but they can grow to nearly 4 m long.

- **As goblin sharks are rarely caught** scientists still don't know much about them.

...FASCINATING FACT...
Goblin sharks probably got their name because of their strange appearance – although they don't really look like goblins!

Crocodile sharks

- **Scientists are still trying** to find out more about the little-known crocodile shark.

- **When fully grown** crocodile sharks are quite small – around 1 m long.

- **The crocodile shark** has huge eyes compared to its body size. They take up almost half its head.

- **Mother crocodile sharks** always give birth to four babies at a time.

- **Small fish**, squid and shrimps are the main diet of the crocodile shark.

- **Humans have only known** about crocodile sharks since 1936, when one was discovered in a fish market in Japan.

- **The crocodile shark's name** comes from its Japanese name, *mizuwani*, meaning 'water crocodile'. It was called this because it has long, pointed teeth and snaps its jaws like a crocodile.

- **Crocodile sharks don't attack people**, but if caught they often bite fishermen on the hand.

- **One of the crocodile shark's closest relatives** is the megamouth shark – even though they're completely different in size and feeding habits.

> ...**FASCINATING FACT**...
> Crocodile sharks cause problems for humans by biting through undersea communications cables.

▶ *Although its big teeth and large eyes make it look threatening, the crocodile shark is actually no bigger than an average-sized dog.*

Shark species

Megamouth sharks

- **One of the most recently discovered** sharks is the megamouth. It probably one of the rarest sharks.

- **The first known megamouth** was caught in 1976, off the islands of Hawaii.

- **The megamouth grows** to over 5 m long. It has a very thick, rounded, heavy body and a huge head.

- **Megamouth sharks are filter-feeders**. They feed at night, cruising along near the ocean surface with their mouths wide open to filter plankton out of the water.

- **During the day**, a megamouth swims down to depths of 200 m or deeper.

- **The megamouth gets its name** because its mouth is so big – up to 1.3 m wide.

- **The megamouth was given the scientific name** *Megachasma pelagios*, which means 'huge yawner of the open sea'.

▼ *It's easy to see how the megamouth got its name. Its mouth is so big, an armchair could fit inside it.*

- **A megamouth shark's mouth** is right at the front of its snout, not underneath as in most sharks.
- **Megamouths have been caught** around the world in the Pacific, Atlantic and Indian Oceans.

...**FASCINATING FACT**...
Fewer than 20 megamouth sharks
have ever been found.

Tiger sharks

- **One of the most dangerous** sharks in the sea is the tiger shark. It will attack almost anything, including humans.

- **Tiger sharks are usually about 3 m long**, but they can grow to 6 m.

- **Young tiger sharks** have stripes to camouflage them and protect them from predators. As a tiger shark gets older, its stripes fade.

- **Tiger sharks** have massive heads with a blunt snout, large eyes and a wide mouth.

- **The diet** of tiger sharks consists of fish, seals, sealions, turtles, shellfish, crabs, seabirds, dolphins, crocodiles, squid and jellyfish. They also take bites out of bigger animals such as whales.

- **Tiger sharks have** even been seen eating other tiger sharks.

- **Many unusual objects**, such as oil drums, tin cans, glass bottles, clothes, rubber tyres, coal, cushions and tools, and even pieces of armour have been found in tiger shark stomachs.

- **The tiger shark is found** in most of the world's warmer seas and oceans.

- **Tiger sharks** sometimes swim into the mouths of rivers.

▶ *A fierce tiger shark closes in on a seal, ready to make a meal of it. Like many other sharks, the tiger shark thrusts its teeth forward to bite. It has several rows of very sharp teeth.*

...FASCINATING FACT...
Tiger sharks might eat metal objects because they give off a slight electrical signal, which the shark can detect with its electrical sense. It probably mistakes them for living things.

Bull sharks

- **Bull sharks are powerful**, ferocious and aggressive hunting sharks.

- **The bull shark gets its name** because its body is thick, stocky and muscular, like a bull.

- **Like the tiger shark**, the bull shark belongs to a family of sharks called requiem sharks.

- **Requiem sharks** probably got their name because of the French word for shark, *requin*.

- **Bull sharks are not especially long** – they usually grow to between 2 to 3 m.

- **Bull sharks** are among the few sharks that can survive in fresh water. They swim hundreds of kilometres up rivers such as the Mississippi, the Amazon and the Zambezi.

- **One group of bull sharks** lives in Lake Nicaragua, a huge lake in Central America.

- **Bull sharks are often known by other names**, depending on where they live – such as the Zambezi river shark or the Nicaragua shark.

- **Especially dangerous** to humans the bull shark lurks in shallow water and rivers, where humans fish, wash and swim.

- **Bull sharks have attacked humans** so often, some experts think they may be the most dangerous sharks of all.

▶ *A bull shark swims along in shallow water with a remora fish below it.*

Blue sharks

- **One of the fastest** sharks in the sea, blue sharks can reach a top speeds of almost 30 km/h.

- **Blue sharks are sleek**, slim, graceful sharks, with a body around 4 m long.

- **The blue shark really is blue**. It's a deep, silvery indigo on top, with a paler underside.

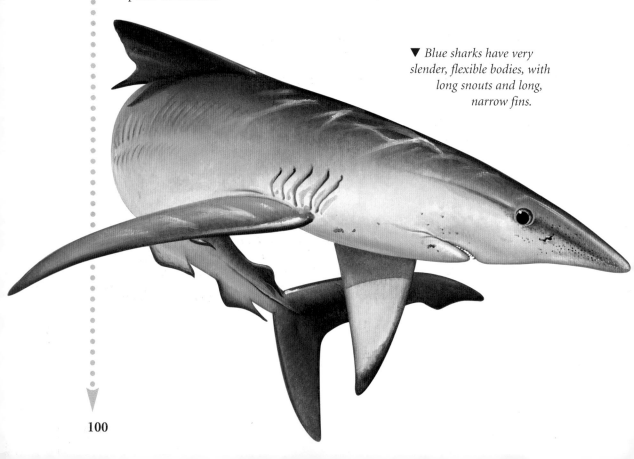

▼ *Blue sharks have very slender, flexible bodies, with long snouts and long, narrow fins.*

- **Blue sharks are famous** for their long journeys. They travel right across oceans, making trips of 3000 km or more.

- **A blue shark can travel** more than 60 km in a day.

- **The blue shark was once** one of the most common sharks, but its population is now falling fast because so many have been caught by humans.

- **Blue sharks are fished** for food, but many more are caught by accident by hooks or nets meant for tuna and swordfish.

- **Experts have estimated** that 6 million blue sharks are caught and killed every year.

- **Blue shark eat mostly squid**, although they will try any kind of fish or other sea creature.

...FASCINATING FACT...
Blue sharks don't normally attack people, but they have been reported to go into feeding frenzies to attack the survivors of sunken ships.

White-tip sharks

- **There are two** quite different sharks that have the name 'white-tip' – the white-tip reef shark and the oceanic white-tip shark.

- **The white-tip reef shark** is a common shark about 1.5 m long.

- **White-tip reef sharks** have distinctive white tips on their tails and dorsal fins.

- **White-tip reef sharks** are often spotted by swimmers and divers because they inhabit in coral reefs, sea caves and shallow water during the day.

- **The white-tip reef shark** lives in warm seas such as the Persian Gulf and the waters around Australia and the Pacific islands.

- **White-tip reef sharks** go hunting at night for squid and octopus.

- **White-tip reef sharks** rarely bother people, except to steal fish from fishing spears.

- **The oceanic white-tip shark** is a large, fast and very common hunting shark, around 3 m long, which lives in the open oceans.

- **The oceanic white-tip shark** sometimes, but not always, has a white or pale grey mark on its dorsal fin.

- **Oceanic white-tips** can be dangerous. They are attracted to shipwrecks and plane wrecks in the sea, and may attack the survivors.

▶ *A white-tip reef shark in its favourite habitat, a shallow coral reef. The white tips on its fins and tail make it easy to identify.*

Black-tip sharks

- **A medium-sized shark** the black-tip reef shark is around 1.5 m long.

- **Like its cousin**, the white-tip, the black-tip reef shark likes warm, shallow water and often lives around coral reefs.

- **Black-tip reef sharks** have black marks on the tips of all their fins.

- **Black-tips** are sometimes simply known as 'black sharks'.

- **The black-tip reef shark** has long, slender teeth ideally suited to snapping up its main prey – fish that live around coral reefs.

- **Scuba divers** and swimmers often encounter black-tip reef sharks, but they're rarely aggressive. They have been known to bite people's legs and feet, but probably only because they mistook them for fish.

- **Another shark**, the spinner shark, is also known as the black-tip shark. It's a completely different species from the black-tip reef shark, and grows to about 2 m long.

- **The black-tip** or spinner shark also has black tips on all its fins.

- **Spinner sharks** get their name because they sometimes leap out of the water and spin around in the air.

◀ *A black-tip reef shark surrounded by coral. Apart from their black-tipped fins, these sharks look similar to their cousins, the white-tip reef sharks.*

. . . **FASCINATING FACT** . . .
Since the Suez Canal was built, black-tip reef sharks have swum through it from the Red Sea, and now live in the Mediterranean Sea too.

Hammerhead sharks

▲ *A hammerhead shark's body shape is similar to that of many other sharks, such as great whites and makos. However, its head is a wide, flat, oblong shape that looks like a hammer when seen from above.*

- **Hammerhead sharks** are probably the strangest-looking sharks of all. Their heads really do look like the ends of hammers.

- **A hammerhead's head** is extremely wide. The shark's eyes are at either end of the 'hammer', making them a very long way apart.

- **Experts think** hammerheads' heads may help them to find food by spreading out their ampullae of Lorenzini (electrical detectors) over a wide area.

- **Seen from the side**, a hammerhead looks similar to a normal shark, as the 'hammer' is so flat and streamlined.

- **There are nine species** of hammerhead. They include great, scalloped, smooth, wingheads, and bonnethead sharks (see bonnethead sharks).

- **The great hammerhead** is the biggest. It can reach 6 m long and has been known to attack humans.

- **Hammerheads go hunting** alone at night for fish, squid, octopuses, crabs, and stingrays. They seem to be immune to the stingray's sting.

- **By day**, hammerheads often swim around in large groups.

- **Hammerheads** have unusually long dorsal fins. They are often seen swimming along with their dorsal fins sticking out of the water.

. . . . **FASCINATING FACT** . . . .
The winghead shark has the widest head of any shark. It can measure as much as half the shark's body length.

107

Bonnethead sharks

- **Bonnetheads** are a type of hammerhead shark.

- **This shark's head** looks less like a hammer, and more like a rounded bonnet or shovel shape.

- **Bonnetheads are the smallest** hammerheads, averaging around 1 m long.

- **Bonnetheads** form huge groups – sometimes there can be thousands of them in a school.

- **The bonnethead shark** is often found in shallow bays and river estuaries. They mainly eat crabs, shrimps and other crustaceans.

- **Scientists think** bonnetheads have complex social systems, with different members of a group having different levels of importance.

- **Bonnetheads** are also called bonnet sharks, bonnetnose sharks, or shovelheads.

- **Fishermen have to be careful** if they grab a bonnethead by the tail, as it can reach up and bite their hand.

- **The scalloped bonnethead** is another type of hammerhead shark. Its bonnet-shaped head has curved or scallop-shaped lines on it.

> ...FASCINATING FACT...
> Dominant bonnethead sharks keep other individuals in their place with behaviour such as head-shaking, jaw-snapping, hunching and butting.

◀ *A bonnethead shark eating a ray.*

109

Lemon sharks

- **The lemon shark** gets its name from its yellowish colour, especially on the underside.

- **Lemon sharks are fish-eating sharks** related to tiger and bull sharks.

- **Lemon sharks grow** up to 3 m long.

- **People sometimes confuse** lemon sharks with bull sharks, as they have a similar shape.

- **Apart from the colour,** you can tell a lemon shark because its two dorsal fins are almost the same size (in most sharks, the first dorsal fin is much bigger).

- **Lemon sharks survive** very well in captivity and might be seen in an aquarium or sealife centre.

- **Since lemon sharks** can be kept in tanks, scientists often use them to do shark experiments.

- **When lemon sharks are young,** they eat small fish, sea worms and shrimps. As they get older, they feed on seabirds, rays and lobsters.

- **Lemon sharks** have been found with stings from stingrays embedded in their mouths.

> **...FASCINATING FACT...**
> When a male and female lemon shark meet up to mate, they swim along side by side, so closely that they can look like a two-headed shark.

▲ *Lemon sharks really are lemon in colour. This helps to distinguish them from bull sharks, which are their close relatives.*

Houndsharks

- **There are over 30** different species of houndsharks.

- **Houndsharks** are a family of smallish sharks around 1.5 m long.

- **Most types of houndsharks** live on shallow seabeds, feeding on shellfish, crabs and lobsters.

- **Instead of sharp biting teeth**, most houndsharks have flat teeth used for crushing their prey.

- **Houndsharks are not the same** as dogfish or dog sharks. They belong to a different shark order, or group.

- **Whiskery sharks** are a type of houndshark with barbels – finger-like organs on their snouts that look like whiskers. They help the shark feel its way along the seabed

- **The tope shark** is a houndshark with a long, pointy snout. It's also called the vitamin shark because it used to be hunted for its liver oil that was used as a health food.

- **Soupfin sharks** are houndsharks too. They get their name because their fins are used to make shark's fin soup – though other sharks are used for this too.

- **Gummy sharks** are another type of houndshark – named because they seem to have have no teeth. Like other houndsharks, they simply have flat, grinding teeth instead of sharp ones.

- **The leopard shark** is an unmistakable species of houndshark. It gets its name from the beautiful, large, leopard-like spots on its back.

▲ *The leopard shark, one of the most beautiful and distinctive of all sharks. Leopard sharks are between 1 m and 2 m long and often swim in groups.*

Weasel sharks and catsharks

- **You can spot a weasel shark** because it looks as if it's had a bite taken out of its tail. This is actually a natural dent in the tail called the 'precaudal pit'.

- **Weasel sharks** are a type of small shark just over 1 m long.

- **There are several different species** of weasel sharks, including the hooktooth, the sickelfin weasel and the snaggletooth.

- **Catsharks** are a separate shark family from weasel sharks. There are over 40 catshark species.

- **Catsharks are less than 1 m in length** and eat small fish and crabs.

- **Catsharks get their name** because their eyes look like a cat's.

- **The lollipop catshark is** an unusual catshark with a very large head.

- **Many catsharks** have beautiful markings. The draughtboard shark, for example, is a catshark with dark and light checkerboard markings, while the chain shark has skin patterns that look like silver chains.

- **Shy-eye sharks** (see shark vision) and swell sharks (see shark shapes) are both types of catsharks.

- **The false catshark** is not a catshark at all. At 3 m long, it's much bigger than a real catshark, and was given its name by mistake.

◀ *Weasel sharks are related to bull and lemon sharks, and have a typical shark shape.*

Dogfish sharks

- **Some of the most common sharks** in the sea are dogfish sharks. They include the piked and the spiny dogfish.

- **Dogfish sharks** are a huge family containing around 80 shark species.

- **Dogfish sharks** usually have spines in front of their dorsal fins and they have no anal fin at all.

- **Dogfish sharks** range in size from under 20 cm long (the spined pygmy shark) to over 6 m long (the Greenland Shark).

- **Millions of dogfish sharks** are caught every year – for their meat, and also for their fins, oil and skin.

- **Spiny dogfish sharks** are ground up to be made into garden fertilizer.

- **Spiny dogfish often cause problems** for fishermen. They tear up fishing nets and eat the fish and steal lobsters from lobster pots.

- **Many species** of dogfish sharks swim together in groups.

- **Dogfish sharks** may have got their name because they form packs, like dogs. In the past, any common type of plant or animal used to be given the name 'dog' – like the dog rose, for example.

> ...FASCINATING FACT...
> In America, spiny dogfish used to be
> caught, dried and burnt as a fuel.

▶ *A group of dogfish sharks on the prowl. They sometimes form schools of hundreds or even thousands of individuals.*

Shark species

Greenland sharks

- **The biggest type** of dogfish shark is the Greenland shark. It grows up to 6.5 m long.

- **Greenland sharks like cold water**. They live in the north Atlantic, around Greenland, Iceland and Canada, and can stand temperatures as low as 2°C.

- **The Greenland shark** is also called the gurry shark and the sleeper shark.

- **The Greenland is known** as the sleeper shark because it is sluggish and swims very slowly.

- **Greenland sharks** have glow-in-the-dark eyes because of luminescent copepods (tiny sea creatures) that live on their eyes. This may help the shark by luring prey towards it.

- **Greenland sharks eat fish**, squid, seals and sealions, as well as scavenging on the dead bodies of whales.

- **Greenlands are found** in water as deep as 1500 m, but in summer they swim up to the surface to find food.

- **Inuit people** traditionally caught Greenland sharks on lines through holes in the ice. They used the skin to make boots and the teeth for knife blades.

- **Fresh Greenland shark** meat is poisonous, but it can be eaten safely if it is boiled several times.

◀ *A Greenland shark swims slowly in the deep, cold water around the Arctic. These sharks are unusual in their choice of habitat as most sharks prefer shallow or warm seas.*

... **FASCINATING FACT** ...
A reindeer was once found inside a dead
Greenland shark's stomach.

119

Dwarf and pygmy sharks

- **The smallest sharks** in the world are dwarf and pygmy sharks. The spined pygmy shark and the dwarf dogshark, or dwarf lanternshark, are both around 18 to 20 cm long.

- **The pygmy shark or slime shark** is larger, but it's still tiny – around 25 cm.

- **Sharks this small** are completely harmless to humans.

- **The spined pygmy shark** lives as deep as 2000 m down during the day, but at night it swims up to hunt in shallower water about 200 m deep.

- **The dwarf dogshark** is also found at great depths – as deep as 1000 m.

- **Dwarf and pygmy sharks** all have luminous undersides (see lighting up).

- **Although dwarf and pygmy sharks** are small, they hunt just like many larger sharks, snapping up fish, shrimps and octopuses.

- **The spined pygmy shark** was first discovered in 1908, when it was caught off the coast of Japan. We now know it lives all around the world. It is also called the cigar shark, because of its small size, slim shape and dark colour.

- **Dwarf and pygmy sharks** are hard to keep in captivity, because they prefer very deep water.

> **... FASCINATING FACT ...**
> The daily vertical migrations of spined pygmy sharks involve
> enormous changes in pressure that most other fish could not survive.

▼ *Working as a group, spined pygmy sharks can attack a sick or injured fish much larger than themselves.*

Cookie-cutter sharks

- **Cookie-cutter sharks** are strange, deep water sharks that are found around the world.

- **There are two species,** the cookie-cutter and the large-tooth cookie-cutter.

- **The large-tooth cookie-cutter** is the smaller of the two, but it has bigger teeth. Its teeth are bigger in relation to its body size than those of any other shark.

- **Cookie-cutters** belong to the dogfish shark family.

- **Cookie-cutter sharks** are brown in colour, with greenish eyes.

- **Instead of eating whole animals**, cookie-cutters take bites out of much bigger sea creatures such as big sharks and whales.

- **To feed, a cookie-cutter shark attaches** itself to its prey by sucking with its mouth. Then it swivels its sharp teeth around in a circle until it has cut out a lump of flesh.

▶ *A close-up view of a cookie-cutter shark's unusual mouth and teeth.*

122

- **Cookie-cutters** themselves are not big – only around 50 cm long. Because they don't need to catch or kill their prey, they can feed on animals that are many times larger than they are.

- **Many sharks, dolphins**, porpoises and whales have permanent, round scars left by cookie-cutters.

▼ *Cookie-cutters open their mouths wide to bite circular lumps out of their prey. They rarely kill their victims.*

> ...FASCINATING FACT...
> Cookie-cutters have been known to take bites
> out of parts of submarines and undersea cables.

Prickly and bramble sharks

- **Almost all sharks** have rough skin (see shark skin), but the skin of prickly and bramble sharks is really rough.

- **The bramble shark** is a deepwater shark that has large, thornlike spikes scattered unevenly all over its body.

- **A bramble shark's spikes** are made of extra-large, extra-sharp denticles (see shark skin).

- **Bramble sharks** grow to about 3 m long.

- **Although they are large**, bramble sharks are rarely seen. This is because they live in deep water and are quite shy.

- **The prickly shark** is a relative of the bramble shark. It looks similar, but has smaller prickles.

- **Prickly sharks grow** to around 4 m long.

- **Prickly dogfish** belong to a separate family. They have deep bodies, and very rough skin rather than long prickles.

- **Though their skin** is tough and prickly, prickly dogfish have strangely soft, spongy lips.

> ...FASCINATING FACT...
> One shark expert described prickly dogfish as
> 'the unloveliest of sharks' because they're so ugly.

▲ *A bramble shark has the prickliest, roughest skin of any shark. Its whole body is scattered with sharp, thorny spikes.*

125

Carpet sharks

- **The carpet sharks** are a varied group of more than 30 different species of sharks.

- **Many carpet sharks** are less than 1 m long, but this group also includes the whale shark, the biggest shark of all.

- **Carpet sharks live** in warm tropical seas, like those around Australia, Indonesia, and Arabia, and usually live in shallow waters around coral reefs and sandbars.

- **Carpet sharks like to lie** still on the seabed. Many of them have a slightly flattened body shape that helps them to camouflage themselves on the sandy or rocky ocean floor.

▼ *The massive whale shark belongs to the carpet shark group. Its relatives include tiny carpet sharks such as the epaulette shark.*

- **Most carpet sharks** feed on seabed-dwelling prey such as crabs, shellfish, octopuses and sea worms.

- **Many carpet sharks** have beautiful mottled, spotted or speckled camouflage markings. They were given their name because these markings often resemble patterned carpets or tapestries

- **Collared carpet sharks** can change colour to match their surroundings, like some other animals such as chameleons and octopuses.

- **Epaulette sharks** are a type of carpet shark. They get their name because they have dark patches on their 'shoulders' – like epaulettes (cloth flaps) on a jacket.

- **Long-tailed carpet sharks** have extra-long tails, with long, fine fins that resemble fronds of seaweed.

- **The barbelthroat carpet shark** has barbels – fleshy finger shapes used for feeling things – on its throat. Only one barbelthroat carpet shark has ever been found.

Wobbegongs

- **Wobbegongs** belong to the carpet shark family.

- **The name 'wobbegong'** was given to these sharks by the Australian Aborigine people. Wobbegongs are often found in shallow, sandy water around the coast of Australia.

- **Wobbegongs** can be quite large – some, like the tass>elled wobbegong, growing up to 4 m long.

- **Wobbegong have wide**, flattened bodies to help them hide on the seabed.

- **A typical wobbegong** has lots of barbels around its mouth.

- **The frilled wobbegong's barbels** are branched and frilly.

- **The tasselled wobbegong** has tassel-like barbels right around its face like a beard.

- **Wobbegong sharks**, also known as wobbies, feed on smaller fish and on other sea creatures such as crabs, octopuses and squid.

- **Wobbegongs have very strong jaws**, and can easily bite off a person's hand or foot.

- **Wobbegongs sometimes attack** people who accidentally step on them. For this reason, they have a reputation as being dangerous, although they are not interested in eating humans and rarely attack unless threatened.

◀ *A wobbegong shark lying in wait for prey on the seabed, disguised among seaweed and coral. When a prey animal, such as a smaller fish, comes close, the wobbegong will rise up and grab it.*

129

Nurse sharks

- **The carpet shark group** includes nurse sharks, although unlike many carpet sharks they don't have blotchy carpet-like markings. Nurse sharks are usually brownish-grey, and sometimes have a few spots.

- **During the day**, nurse sharks often lie around on the seabed in groups. This has given them a reputation for being sluggish and lazy.

- **At night**, nurse sharks wake up and go hunting.

- **Nurse sharks** can reach 4 m long, but most are nearer 3 m in length.

- **No one knows how** nurse sharks got their name. They may have been named by someone who saw a nurse shark near its young.

- **Nurse sharks** have two fleshy barbels hanging down underneath their noses.They use them to smell and feel their way along the seabed as they search for prey.

- **Crabs, lobsters and sea urchins** are the preferred food of nurse sharks. They have flat, grinding teeth for crushing up shells.

- **If a nurse shark** bites you, it hangs on with a clamplike grip that's very painful (though not deadly). It can be impossible to shake the shark off unless you can get it out of the water, where it can't breathe.

- **As they survive** well in aquariums, nurse sharks can be used in shark intelligence experiments.

▶ *A diver creeps close to a nurse shark to get a good look. This shark is hiding in a gap in a coral reef, a favourite habitat of nurse sharks.*

...FASCINATING FACT...

Divers sometimes grab nurse sharks' tails, hoping for a ride.
The sharks don't like this and may turn around and bite.

Blind sharks

- **The carpet shark group** includes the blind shark. This shark is not actually blind at all.

- **When they are caught** and pulled out of the water, blind sharks close their eyes tightly and appear to have no eyes.

- **Blind sharks** live off the coast of Australia and are often found in shallow water near the shore. They hide in caves or crevices during the day and hunt at night.

- **There are two species** of blind shark. One is simply known as the blind shark, while the other is called Colclough's shark or the bluegray carpet shark.

- **The blind shark is yellow underneath** and brownish on top, with pale spots.

- **At 1.3 m in length**, the blind shark is slightly bigger than Colclough's shark, which is just under 1 m long.

- **Young blind sharks** have dark stripes or bands across their bodies, which fade as they grow older.

- **Colclough's shark**, as its other name suggests, is blueish-grey in colour.

- **Both types** of blind shark feed by snuffling along the seabed for cuttlefish, shellfish and crabs.

- **Blind sharks** have large spiracles (see how sharks breathe). These help them breathe even when their snouts are buried in the muddy seabed to find food.

▶ *Blind sharks can see perfectly well in their natural habitat.*

Tawny and zebra sharks

- **Part of the carpet shark group**, tawny and zebra sharks are related to nurse, blind and whale sharks.

- **At 3 m in length**, the tawny shark is quite large. It lives in warm tropical seas close to the shore.

- **The tawny shark** is also known as the spitting shark because it spits out water as a defence if captured.

- **After spitting**, the tawny shark is said to grunt. It is one of the few sharks thought to make a noise.

- **The zebra shark** is another medium-sized carpet shark that grows up to 3 m long.

- **Distinctive** dark and pale stripes give zebra sharks their name – but they only have these when they are young. As they become adults, the stripes separate into blotches.

- **A zebra shark's egg cases** are a deep purplish-brown and have tufts of hair on them to help them lodge firmly among rocks and seaweed.

- **Like thresher sharks**, zebra sharks have very long tails (see thresher sharks).

- **Zebra sharks** have long, hard ridges running all the way down the backs and sides of their bodies. This helps divers to recognize them immediately.

> ...FASCINATING FACT...
> The tawny shark has a powerful suck. It can use its mouth to
> suck prey such as fish and octopuses out of their hiding places.

▼ *As a young zebra shark grows, its stripes break up into spots or blobs. This adult zebra shark shows how some of its spots were once connected to form stripes.*

Whale sharks

- **The carpet shark group** also includes the whale shark.

- **Closest relatives** of the whale shark are wobbegongs and nurse sharks – not other filter-feeders like basking sharks and megamouths.

- **Whale sharks** are the biggest sharks in the world. Their average length is 10 to 12 m long – as long as a six or seven adult humans lying end-to-end.

- **The filter-feeding** whale shark sieves tiny plankton out of the water.

- **To feed**, whale sharks swim along with their massive mouths open. A whale shark's mouth can be 1.5 m across.

- **A whale shark** has around 3000 tiny teeth, but it doesn't use them to eat with. Instead, it uses bristles in its gills to trap its food.

- **Whale sharks** are covered with pale stripes and spots.

- **Scientists think** some whale sharks could live to be 100 years old or more.

- **Whale sharks** might look dangerous, but they're harmless to humans.

> ...FASCINATING FACT...
> A whale shark's skin is around 10 cm thick,
> making it the thickest skin in the world.

◄ *As a whale shark cruises along filtering
plankton out of the water, it sometimes
swallows larger fish. Fish as big as tuna,
which can grow to 4 m long, have been seen
disappearing into whale sharks' mouths.*

Hornsharks

- **The relatively small** hornshark has its own order, or shark group. It reaches 1.0 m to 1.5 m in length.

- **Hornsharks get their name** because they have poisonous spines, or horns, in front of both their dorsal fins.

- **Because of their large**, rounded heads, hornsharks are also called bullhead sharks.

- **Hornsharks have piglike snouts** and large lumps above their eyes that look like eyebrows.

- **Crabs and sea urchins** are the preferred food of hornsharks. They have sharp biting teeth at the front of their mouths, and flat chewing teeth at the back.

- **Hornsharks are only found** in the Pacific and Indian Oceans.

- **After laying**, the female hornshark takes each egg case in her mouth and jams it into a rock crevice before leaving it to hatch. The eggcases are spiral-shaped.

- **Spines from hornsharks** are sometimes made into jewellery.

- **The Port Jackson shark** is a type of hornshark, named after it was found in the bay of Port Jackson, Australia.

> ...FASCINATING FACT...
> Some hornsharks have red-stained teeth
> because of all the sea urchins they eat.

▼ *Hornsharks use the sharp spines near their fins to defend themselves against any predators that try to catch them.*

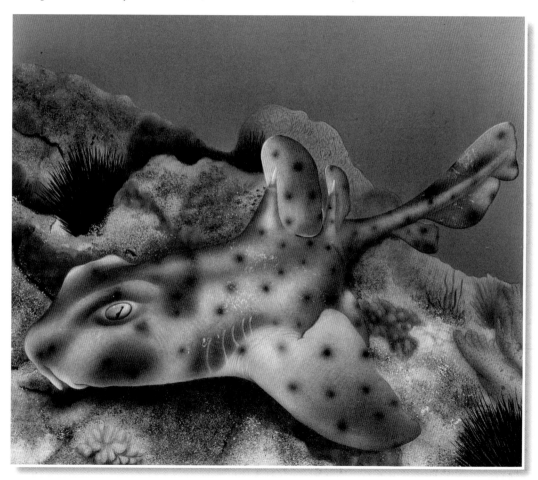

Angel sharks

- **The angel shark order** contains about ten species of sharks. They get their name because of their wide, winglike fins.

- **Monkfish** is another name for angel sharks, because people used to think their fins looked like a monk's robes.

- **Another name** for angel sharks is sand devils. because they lie on the seabed and sometimes bite people who tread on them.

- **Angel sharks** have very flattened bodies. Most are around 1.5 m long.

- **The biggest angel shark** is the Japanese angel shark, which reaches 2 m long. It is hunted for food and was once also used to make shagreen (sharkskin sandpaper).

- **By burying themselves** on the sandy seabed, angel sharks are hidden from passing fish and shellfish. They leap out to catch their prey with their small but sharp teeth.

- **An angel shark can lie** in wait for over a week until the right food comes past.

- **Like wobbegongs** and other bottom-dwelling sharks, angel sharks are camouflaged with spotted, speckled skin patterns.

- **In some countries**, angel sharks are served as a delicacy in expensive restaurants, where they are always called monkfish.

- **Angel sharks are viviparous** – they give birth to live babies. There are usually around ten pups in a litter.

▲ *An angel shark in its preferred habitat, the shallow, sandy seabed. This shark is clearly visible, but most can be very hard to spot when they are lying on the sea floor.*

Saw sharks

- **Part of an order** of five species of shark, saw sharks have flat heads and long, saw-shaped snouts.

- **A saw shark's snout** is called a rostrum. It is pointed and has teeth of various sizes, called rostral teeth, sticking out all the way around it.

- **At around 1 m** in length, saw sharks are relatively small.

- **For their size**, saw sharks' 'saws' are very long compared to other sharks' snouts. The snout of a longnose saw shark can make up half its total body length.

- **Saw sharks use** their saws for digging up prey such as shellfish from the seabed. Then they slash and jab at the prey before eating it.

- **The two long barbels** halfway along its snout help the saw shark feel its way along the seabed.

- **People sometimes** eat saw sharks in Japan and Australia.

- **Most saw sharks are grey**, but one species, the Japanese saw shark, is a muddy brown.

- **Saw sharks should not** be confused with sawfish, which are a type of ray (see rays).

... **FASCINATING FACT** ...
Saw sharks aren't usually seen near the shore.
They prefer to live at depths of up to 400 m.

▶ *A saw shark hunting for food using its snout and sensitive barbels, which can feel, smell and taste its fishy prey.*

Frilled sharks

- **The frilled shark** is the only species in its family.

- **A strange looking shark**, the frilled shark has big, frilly gill slits – the first pair reach right around its head like a collar.

- **The long, thin body** of the frilled shark reaches up to 2 m in length.

- **Frilled sharks** only have one dorsal fin, instead of two as in most sharks. This fin is positioned far back towards the shark's tail.

- **Because of its snakelike appearance**, the frilled shark is sometimes mistaken for an eel or a sea snake.

- **Found in the cold**, deep water of the Pacific and Atlantic Oceans, frilled sharks feed on octopuses and squid.

- **With three sharp points** on each tooth, frilled sharks have very unusual teeth. This is one of the features that is used to identify this rare shark.

- **Frilled sharks** have six gill slits on each side. This is very unusual – only a few sharks have more than five (including the frilled shark's relatives, six-gill and seven-gill sharks, and the six-gill saw shark).

- **Scientists have found** that after female frilled sharks mate, they are pregnant for as long as three years.

- **People used to think** that the frilled shark had been extinct for millions of years, as it was only known from ancient fossils. Living frilled sharks were first discovered in the late 19th century.

▶ *A frilled shark swimming in deep water. This species of shark is extremely rare.*

Shark relatives

- **Sharks are closely related** to two other groups of fish – the batoids and the chimaeras.

- **The batoids include** rays, skates and sawfish.

- **Batoids range** from plate-sized skates to giant manta rays more than 8 m across.

- **There are more than** 500 species of batoids – more than there are species of sharks.

  - **Most batoids have** wide, flat heads and bodies, and long tapering tails. They look similar to some types of sharks, such as angel sharks.

    - **Like some sharks**, batoids spend most of their time on the seabed.

      - **Batoids feed on** bottom-dwelling sea creatures such as clams, shrimps and flatfish.

◄ *The giant manta ray has enormous winglike pectoral fins and a narrow tail.*

▲ *An electric ray, a type of batoid, resting its flat body on the seabed. Its eyes are on the top of its body, as in angel sharks and other flat-bodied sharks.*

- **Because sharks are often difficult** to catch and keep in captivity, scientists often study batoids instead. They are so similar to sharks that they can provide clues to how sharks live.

- **Chimaeras are a group** of fish that are like sharks in some ways and more like bony fish in other ways.

- **Like sharks**, batoids and chimaeras have light, flexible skeletons made of cartilage, instead of having bones like other fish.

147

Rays

- **Close relatives** of sharks, rays are a type of batoid (see shark relatives).

- **With their huge winglike fins**, some ray species wider than they are long.

- **A ray swims** using rippling motions of its fins and looks as if it is 'flying' along.

- **Many rays have** a long, whiplike tail. Unlike sharks, they don't use their tails to push themselves through the water.

- **Rays live in seas** and oceans all around the world, from shallows near the shore to seabeds 3000 m deep.

- **Rays have eyes** on the tops of their heads and large spiracles to breathe through. This means they can still see and breathe easily while lying on the seabed.

- **Most rays are ovoviviparous** – they give birth to live young that have hatched from eggs inside their mothers' bodies.

- **Many rays are solitary** and like to live alone. However some, like golden cow-nosed rays, form huge groups of thousands of individuals.

- **Some rays**, such as the mangrove stingray and the huge manta ray, can leap right out of the water.

- **Like sharks**, all rays are carnivores. Some hunt for fish or shellfish, while others are filter-feeders.

▶ *Two different ray species: the huge manta ray, which has a dark upper side and a paler underside, and the smaller spotted eagle ray, which has a white underside and spots on top. Both are found in tropical waters around the world.*

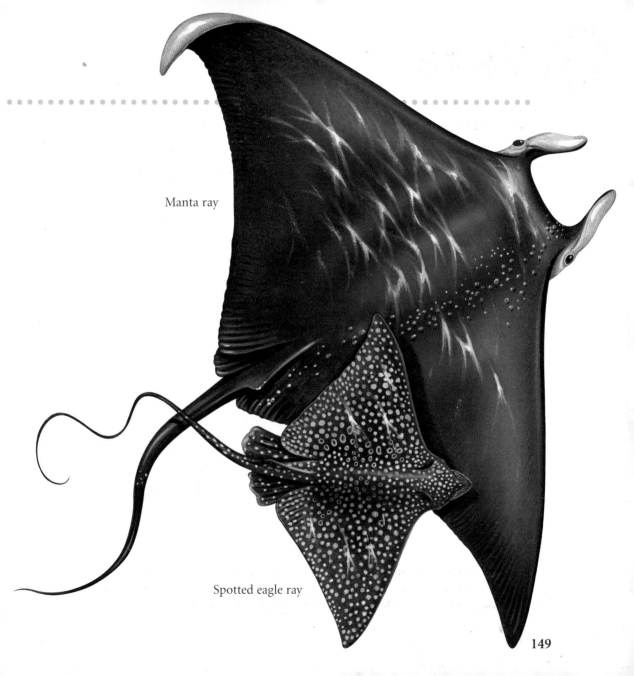

Manta ray

Spotted eagle ray

149

Types of rays

- **The biggest ray** of all is the manta ray. It is usually about 7 m wide by 7 m long (including the tail). The biggest are nearly 9 m wide.

- **The manta ray is a filter-feeder**, like the basking and whale sharks. It sucks in seawater and filters tiny plankton out of it.

- **Stingrays have a poisonous spine** (or sometimes two or three) in the middle of their tails. They are used mainly to defend themselves against attackers.

- **River stingrays**, unlike other rays, live in fresh water. They are found in rivers in Africa and South America, especially the river Amazon.

- **Round stingrays** have almost completely round, flat bodies, like dinner plates.

- **Electric rays** can generate electricity to give other animals a powerful electric shock. It can be used to put off predators, or to stun prey.

- **Short-nose electric rays** include some of the smallest rays, at less than 20 cm across.

- **The blind electric ray** is almost completely blind. It relies on its sense of electrical detection, which works like radar, to find prey.

- **Spotted eagle rays** are covered with beautiful pale spots on a dark background.

> ...FASCINATING FACT...
> Stingray stings have often been used around
> the world to make pointed weapons.

▼ Inside a manta ray's mouth are five pairs of gill arches, which filter food from the water. The food particles get trapped in a spongy material between the gill arches, while the water passes out through the ray's gill slits.

Sawfish

▲ *A sawfish (a type of ray) can be told apart from a saw shark (a type of shark) by the shape of its snout. While saw sharks have pointed 'saws', a sawfish snout is the same width all the way along, with a gently curved tip.*

- **Another type** of ray is the sawfish.
- **Sawfish get their name** from their long, sawlike snouts, which are edged with sharp teeth like the teeth on a saw.
- **The green sawfish** grows to over 7 m long – longer than a great white shark.
- **The saw can account** for up to one-third of a sawfish's whole length.
- **Like rays**, sawfish have flattened bodies, but they look more like sharks than most rays do.
- **A sawfish uses its saw** to poke around for prey on the seabed and to slice into shoals of fish before eating them.

- **When young sawfish are born**, their snouts are soft and enclosed in a covering of skin. This protects the inside of the mother's body from being injured by the sharp teeth. After birth, the protective skin soon falls off and the saw becomes harder.

- **The large-tooth sawfish** sometimes swims up rivers in Australia.

- **Although sawfish** look quite like saw sharks (see saw sharks), they are not the same at all. Sawfish are much bigger. They also have longer saws for their body size and no barbels.

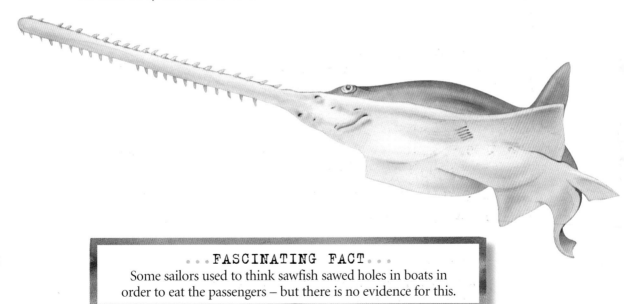

...FASCINATING FACT...
Some sailors used to think sawfish sawed holes in boats in order to eat the passengers – but there is no evidence for this.

153

Skates

- **A relative of sharks**, skates are similar to rays (see rays), although they tend to have a straighter edges to the front of their pectoral fins and shorter tails.

- **Most types of skate** live in deep water, as far as 3000 m down. Their bodies are very flat.

- **Skates usually lie** on the seabed waiting for prey such as crabs and shrimps to come close.

- **As its mouth** is on its underside, the skate does not lunge at its prey. Instead it swim over it and grasps it from above.

- **Like some sharks**, skates lay eggs with tough, protective cases around them.

- **Skate eggcases** have stiff spikes on them to help them stick into the seabed, and a sticky coating so that they soon become covered with sand or pebbles as a form of camouflage.

- **Skates are a very popular food** with people – especially the fins, which are called 'skate wings'.

- **The largest skates** include common and barndoor skates. They can reach 2 m to 3 m long (about the size of a large door).

- **The Texas skate** has two large spots, one on each wing. This may be a disguise that helps the skate stay safe by making it look like the eyes of a much bigger animal.

> ...FASCINATING FACT...
> Sailors used to collect skates, dry them, twist them into
> strange shapes and sell them as miniature sea monsters.

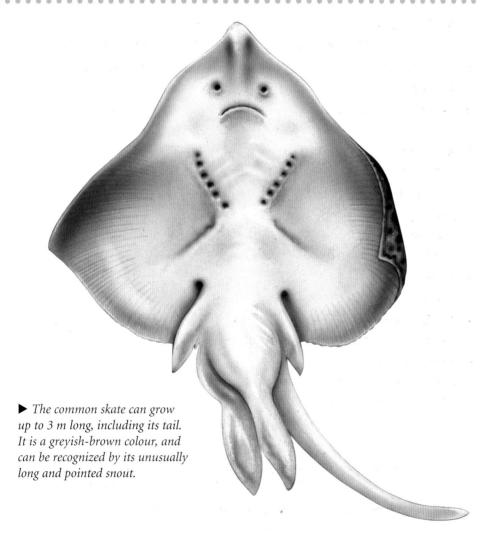

▶ *The common skate can grow up to 3 m long, including its tail. It is a greyish-brown colour, and can be recognized by its unusually long and pointed snout.*

Chimaeras

- **Although related to sharks**, chimaeras are not true sharks or rays. They belong to a separate group of cartilaginous fish.

- **Various types** of chimaeras are also known as ratsharks, ratfish, ghost sharks, spookfish and even 'ghouls'.

- **Chimaeras grow** to a maximum of around 2 m long, but most are smaller, from 60 cm to 100 cm long. Like rays and some sharks, many chimaeras have very long tails, which can make up a large part of their body length.

- **Feeding on small fish** and octopuses, chimaeras usually live on the seabed.

- **Chimaeras are so called** because they look like a combination of different types of fish.

- **Like some sharks**, chimaeras have a spine in front of their dorsal fin.

- **Another sharklike feature** of chimaeras is that they lay eggs in eggcases. Chimaera eggcases can be very big – up to 40 cm long.

- **Chimaeras have a covering** over their gill slits. Sharks and rays do not have this, but other kinds of fish do.

- **Unlike sharks** and rays, chimaeras swim very slowly, and have fine, ribbed fins.

▶ *A ratfish, a type of chimaera, swimming close to the seabed. The chimneys in the background are hydrothermal vents, where hot water and minerals stream out from under the ocean floor. Ratfish are often found near these vents.*

......FASCINATING FACT......
In Greek mythology, a chimaera was a monster that was part
lion, part goat and part snake.

Sharks and humans

- **Sharks have been around** for much longer than humans have.

- **It's a natural instinct** for people to be scared of sharks, as some of them are fierce hunters.

- **However**, people are more dangerous to sharks than the other way around.

- **Some sharks**, such as Greenland sharks and angel sharks, are among the easiest fish to catch with a hook or fishing spear – people have probably been eating them for thousands of years.

- **As well as for food**, people hunt sharks for all kinds of useful products such as sharkskin leather and liver oil (see more uses for sharks).

- **People in the Pacific islands** used shark teeth to make tools and weapons as long as 5000 years ago.

- **In the 5th century** BC, the ancient Greek historian Herodotus wrote about how sharks attacked sailors when ships sank during battles at sea.

- **The ancient Greek** scientist Aristotle studied sharks in the 4th century BC, and was one of the first to notice that they were different in many ways from other fish.

- **Sharks are sometimes** described as cruel, heartless, vicious or mean killers. In fact, like most meat-eating animals, sharks only kill in order to survive.

> ...FASCINATING FACT...
> The word 'shark' is sometimes used to
> mean a ruthless person or a thief.

▼ Although people are scared of sharks, they are very interested in them too. This photographer is using an underwater camera to get the best possible close-up photo of a great white shark.

Fear of sharks

● **Many people** are very scared of being bitten or even eaten by a shark while swimming in the sea.

● **The great white shark** is the most feared shark.

● **Other large, fierce** sharks such as tiger and bull sharks also terrify people.

● **Although sharks can** be dangerous, our fear of them is completely out of proportion to how dangerous they are. Shark attacks are actually very rare.

◄ *A promotional poster for the film* Jaws, *about a killer great white shark. This poster exaggerates the shark by making it look much bigger than it really is.*

- **One reason** people find sharks so frightening is that they live underwater, so it is hard to see them.

- **Another reason** may be their big teeth and eyes that seem to show no emotion. Humans instinctively prefer 'cute' animals to fierce-looking ones.

- **In the past**, sailors were famous for being superstitious. Their tales about sharks and shark attacks were probably exaggerated and scared people more than they needed to.

- **Fear of sharks** has been increased by books and films about shark attacks. There are many more films and books about killer sharks than there are about other dangerous animals.

- **Because shark attacks are rare**, when they do happen they appear in the news and everyone hears about them. This makes sharks seem more dangerous than they really are.

> ...FASCINATING FACT...
> People are more likely to be killed by a hippo, crocodile,
> dangerous water current, or lightning, than by a shark.

Shark attacks

- **Around the world**, there are fewer than 100 reported cases every year of sharks attacking humans who are swimming or surfing in the sea.

- **Of these attacks**, fewer than 20 result in someone dying.

- **Most shark attacks happen** in shallow, warm water near the shore, because that's where sharks and swimmers are likely to be in the same place at the same time.

- **The worst shark tragedy** ever was in 1945, during World War II. A US warship was torpedoed and sank in the South Pacific, leaving 1000 crew members in the water. Before they could be rescued, over 600 of them had been eaten by sharks.

- **In the summer of 1969**, four people were killed in shark attacks within two weeks off the coast of New Jersey, USA.

- **The areas with the most** shark attacks are the coasts of eastern North America, South Africa, and eastern Australia.

- **Sharks usually only attack** if they feel threatened – for example a wobbegong may bite if it gets stepped on – or if sharks mistake a human for prey, such as a seal.

- **Most shark attacks** happen in summer and during the afternoon.

- **Men are about ten times** more likely than women to be attacked by a shark. This is probably because a greater number of men go surfing and swim far further out in the sea.

▲ *Of the few shark attacks that do take place, some happen to people who are surfing. This may be because from below, a surfboard looks similar to a seal or a turtle – the favourite foods of large hunting sharks such as great whites.*

...FASCINATING FACT...
Experts have found that if a shark does take a bite of human flesh, it often spits it out or vomits it up later.

163

Survival stories

- **In 1749**, 14-year-old Brook Watson lost a leg to a shark while swimming at Havana, Cuba. He later became Mayor of London and was famous for his wooden leg.

- **Rodney Fox** was grabbed by a great white while taking part in a spear-fishing contest in Australia in 1963. His body was bitten right open, but he survived and went on to become a shark expert.

▲ *Shark attack survivor and world-famous shark expert Rodney Fox shows photographs of the injuries he suffered when he was badly bitten by a great white shark.*

- **A great white shark** bit off undersea photographer Henri Bource's leg while he was diving off Australia in 1964. He was soon back at work in the same job, and four years later another shark bit his artificial leg!

- **In 1996**, surfer Joey Hanlon was attacked by a great white while surfing in California, USA. The shark bit into his torso, but he recovered after being given over 300 stitches.

- **Another surfer**, John Forse, was on his surfboard in Oregon, USA in 1998 when a great white shark grabbed his leg and pulled him deep underwater. He escaped by hitting the shark's dorsal fin until it let go.

- **13-year-old** Bethany Hamilton had her left arm bitten off by a tiger shark while surfing in Hawaii in 2003. She was surfing again within months.

- **Fishermen** often get bitten on the hands by sharks they have caught. Most of these shark bites are minor and go unreported.

- **Shark attack survivors** are often left with huge semicircular scars from the shark's teeth.

- **Today**, shark attack victims are more likely to survive than they used to be, thanks to fast boats and modern treatments such as blood transfusions.

...FASCINATING FACT...

In 2004, while snorkelling in Australia, Luke Tresoglavic was bitten by a small wobbegong that refused to let go. Tresoglavic had to swim to shore and drive to get help with the shark still attached to his leg.

Shark safety

- **Humans** have developed several ways to try to stay safe from shark attacks.

- **Swimming beaches** in shark areas are sometimes surrounded with strong nets to keep sharks out.

- **Special chainmail diving suits** can protect divers from sharks' teeth, although the body can still be crushed by a shark bite.

- **Some ships carry shark screens** – floating sacks that shipwreck survivors can climb inside. The screen disguises a person's shape and hides their scent, making them less likely to attract sharks.

- **Anti-shark weapons** can be used to scare sharks away. They include electrical prods that confuse a shark's electrical sense, and bangsticks, which are like underwater guns.

- **Some people have tried** to banish sharks by releasing chemicals they don't like the smell of into the water.

- **Some divers in shark areas** wear striped diving suits for camouflage, so that it's harder for sharks to see them.

- **You shouldn't swim** in a shark zone if you have a cut or wound on your body. The blood could attract sharks.

- **If you see a large shark** when you're in the sea, the safest thing to do is to stay calm, avoid splashing about, and swim steadily towards the shore.

> ...FASCINATING FACT...
> If you are ever attacked by a shark, you may
> be able to scare it off by punching its snout.

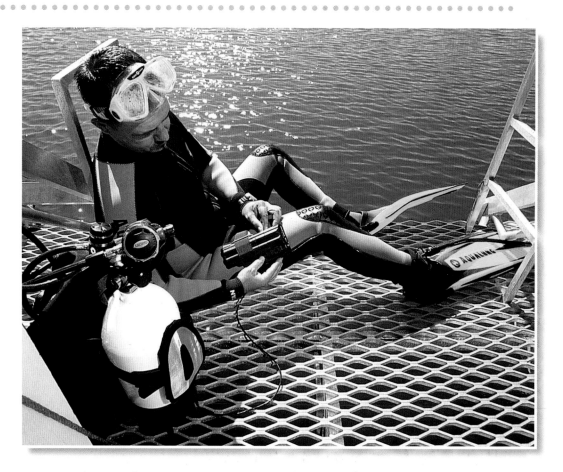

▲ *A diver attaching an anti-shark device to his leg before diving. This device works by giving out electrical signals that sharks find unpleasant, so they stay away.*

Dangerous sharks

- **The great white shark** is often thought to be the most dangerous shark because it is most often identified in shark attacks. This is because it is well-known and easy to recognize. It is blamed for up to half of all serious shark attacks.

- **As well as biting** humans, great whites have been known to attack small boats.

- **Why are great whites so deadly?** It may be partly because they love eating seals and sealions, which look similar to humans in size and shape. The sharks simply get confused and attack the wrong prey.

- **Many experts** think bull sharks are actually more dangerous than great whites – but they are not well-known as killers because they are harder to spot and identify.

- **After bull sharks attack**, they often escape unseen.

- **Not all dangerous sharks** are fast hunters. Nurse sharks and wobbegongs are usually placid and sluggish – but they can bite suddenly and hard if disturbed or annoyed.

- **Sharks with spines**, such as horn and dogfish sharks, are not deadly but often inflict painful injuries on people.

- **Stingrays**, which are related to sharks, can be killers – a few people die every year from their venom.

- **Sharks often bite** then swim away fast, making it hard to tell what species they are.

- **Huge basking sharks** and manta rays, though they don't bite, can be dangerous if they leap out of the water and land on a small boat.

▶ *A great white shark showing how deadly its bite could be as it mouths the bars of an underwater shark-watching cage.*

Harmless sharks

- **The vast majority** of shark species are not interested in eating humans and never attack them.

- **Many sharks**, such as pygmy and zebra sharks, are so small they could not kill or eat a human even if they wanted to.

- **Most sharks can bite**, but will only do so if they themselves are attacked, caught or threatened.

- **Filter-feeders** such as whale sharks have very big mouths, but their throats are narrow, so they can't swallow a human.

- **Whale sharks** are often very friendly. They let snorkellers come close and even touch them.

- **Even big, dangerous sharks** such as the great white can get used to humans and become friendly enough to be stroked and tickled.

- **Harmless sharks** such as basking sharks are sometimes killed because they are mistaken for great whites or other dangerous sharks.

- **At some aquariums** and sealife centres, visitors can pay to climb into the tank with non-dangerous sharks.

- **Many shark scientists**, experts and photographers spend huge amounts of time with sharks without ever getting bitten.

- **Some people** even keep small sharks at home in fishtanks, although this is very difficult to do.

▶ *A diver releasing a small nurse shark into the wild after rescuing it from captivity. Sometimes, sharks that are caught and kept in captivity seem harmless until they grow too big, and have to be released.*

Shark fishing

- **Important species** for fishing include thresher sharks and various types of dogfish.

- **Most of the sharks** caught are used as food, though sharks have many other uses too (see more uses for sharks).

- **Smaller sharks** such as the lesser spotted dogfish are caught by trawlers – boats that drag, or trawl huge fishing nets along behind them.

- **Flat, bottom-dwelling sharks** such as angel sharks can be caught by a diver using a fishing spear to stab through the shark onto the seabed.

- **Sea anglers** go fishing for sharks as a sport. Many coastal tourist resorts have special boats that take tourists sportfishing for sharks and other large fish.

- **Sport fishermen** like to catch fast-swimming species, such as porbeagle and mako sharks, because they struggle a lot when they are hooked and so provide the most entertainment.

- **Whale sharks** and other species are sometimes hunted just for their fins. After the fins are cut off, the rest of the shark is thrown back into the sea to die.

- **Millions of sharks** are caught by accident every year in nets meant for other sea creatures, such as squid.

- **Sharks are often** caught and killed just because there is a small risk that they might bite someone.

- **Humans catch** around 100 million sharks every year.

▶ *A sport fisherman lands a medium-sized shark that he has caught using a fishing rod and line. Sharks caught for sport are often thrown back into the sea alive, but they may be killed and eaten, or preserved and stuffed to display as a trophy.*

Sharks as food

▲ *A worker preparing a huge pile of shark fins to be used in shark's-fin soup. Many of the sharks were probably killed just for their fins. The rest of the shark is thrown away.*

- **Sharks** are a nutritious food because their flesh is very lean and full of protein. It often tastes good, too.

- **However**, many people don't like the idea of eating sharks, so when they are sold as food, sharks' names are often changed to things such as 'grayfish' or 'huss'.

- **In Japan** you can buy canned shark, smoked shark and shark fishcakes.

- **Raw shark** is eaten as part of traditional Japanese sashimi dishes.

- **Shark's-fin soup**, popular in Asia, is made by boiling shark fins to extract the gluey cartilage rods, which are the soup's main ingredient.

- **In the UK**, fish and chips is a popular takeaway meal. This fish is often a shark, the spiny dogfish – sold as 'rock salmon'.

- **As well as eating sharks** ourselves, we use many shark species to make pet food. Even cat or dog food that is labelled as another flavour, such as chicken or tuna, will probably also contain shark meat from a common shark species such as the spiny dogfish.

- **Some types of Muslims** do not eat sharks as their religion forbids them to eat fish without scales.

- **Shark flesh goes off very fast.** It has to be eaten when fresh, or preserved by canning, smoking or pickling soon after being caught.

...FASCINATING FACT...
In Iceland, people eat dried, slightly rotted
Greenland shark – a dish known as hakarl.

More uses for sharks

- **Polished shark skin** leather was once used to cover books and scientific objects such as telescopes.

- **Some species**, such as the spotted wobbegong, are still hunted for their skin. It's made into things such as shoes and handbags.

- **The ancient Greeks** used burnt angel shark skin to treat skin diseases, and shocks from electric rays as a painkiller during operations.

- **Parts of sharks** are often made into health food supplements – such as shark liver oil tablets, which contain E and A vitamins. Some people around the world even believe that eating parts of sharks can give you a shark's strength and courage, but there is no evidence for this.

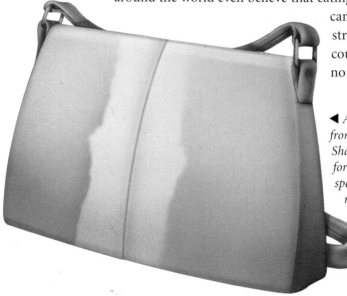

◄ *A handbag made from shark skin leather. Sharks that are hunted for their skin are usually species with beautiful mottled or speckled markings, such as the carpet shark.*

176

...FASCINATING FACT...
Shagreen – shark leather that still has its rough denticles – was
used in the past to make non-slip grips for sword handles.

- **Shark liver oil** is also used in some cosmetics, candles and paints.

- **Shark cartilage** is used to make a medicine for treating burns.

- **A type of medicine** for heart disease is made from chemicals extracted from sharks' blood.

- **Scientists have worked out** how to use shark corneas (the transparent protective covering in front of the eye) to make cornea transplants for humans.

- **Sharks' teeth** are often made into necklaces and other jewellery.

▶ *Vitamin pills made from shark liver oil are thought to help heal wounds and prevent diseases such as flu.*

177

Shark tourism

▲ *A diver has a close encounter with a great white shark while cage-diving. The great white is probably the most exciting shark of all for enthusiasts to see.*

- **People like to see** sharks in close-up, partly because they are feared and exciting, and also because many people enjoy watching all kinds of wildlife.
- **In coastal areas** around the world, tourists pay to see real sharks in their natural habitat.

- **Going on a holiday** or trip to watch sharks is an example of wildlife tourism. Ecotourism is tourism that is used to help preserve wild habitats and species. A percentage of the money paid by the ecotourists is used for conservation work.

- **To view dangerous sharks**, tourists go cage-diving. They are lowered into the sea inside a protective metal cage.

- **Cage-diving** with blue sharks is popular off the coast of the eastern USA. People can view great whites in Australia and South Africa.

- **People go swimming** with sharks too. Tour operators organize dives and snorkelling trips to see species such as hammerhead, reef and whale sharks.

- **On shark-feeding tours**, tourists go scuba-diving to the seabed, where the guide opens a bucket of frozen fish to attract medium-sized species such as white-tip reef sharks.

- **Sharks also attract visitors** to sealife centres and aquariums, where you can often walk through the shark tank in an underwater tunnel.

- **Undersea photographers** use special underwater cameras to take pictures of tourists with sharks as part of the experience.

... FASCINATING FACT ...
Unlike dolphins and sealions, sharks don't perform for an audience.
It's very hard to train a shark to learn complicated tricks.

Sharks in captivity

- **Most shark species** are very difficult to keep in captivity. They need special tanks with lots of space.

- **For a shark to survive** in captivity the water has to be exactly the right saltiness and temperature so that it matches the shark's natural habitat.

- **For this reason**, many aquariums only keep sharks that come from their own local area. The further a shark is from home, the harder it is to recreate the conditions it is used to.

- **The sharks that do best** in captivity are sand tiger and lemon sharks and smaller sharks such as houndsharks and lesser spotted dogfish.

- **Captive sharks** can suffer from diseases such as goitre, caused by a lack of minerals they need to stay healthy.

- **Sharks in captivity** seem to eat less than those in the wild. In captivity they do not expend so much energy in finding food or in day-to-day living.

- **The tiger shark** is one of the few large, fierce sharks to have survived a long time in captivity. They have been kept in aquariums for up to five years.

- **To be transported** from the wild to an aquarium, sharks have to be carried in special holding tanks that are transported on trucks or planes.

- **In 1998**, a group of sandbar sharks died in an aquarium in the UK after getting too cold when their flight was delayed at Amsterdam airport.

...FASCINATING FACT...
One great white shark kept in an aquarium was so distressed that it
kept swimming into the walls of the tanks, and had to be released.

▼ *Tourists at one of the world's largest aquariums, at Okinawa in Japan, gaze at a
7 m-long whale shark. Until recently, it has been almost impossible to keep whale sharks
in captivity as they are so big.*

Sharks in trouble

▲ *A fishing boat off the Philippines carries home a haul of shark fins. Fishermen continue to catch endangered sharks just for their fins, even though this is against the law, because they can make so much money by selling them to make shark's-fin fin soup.*

- **There are far fewer sharks** than there used to be. The populations of many species are falling fast and some are in danger of dying out.

- **This is mainly because** of human activities such as hunting and fishing.

- **Overfishing may mean** that shark populations can't recover. For example, porbeagle sharks have been overfished to make shark's-fin soup.

- **In the second half** of the 20th century, shark fishing increased as shark meat, health foods and shark's-fin soup became more popular.

- **Sharks are also in demand** because other fish such as cod have become scarce, having also been overfished.

- **Many sharks** are killed when they get caught in nets put up to protect swimmers from shark attacks.

- **Sharks caught** for sport are usually released, but often die from exhaustion soon afterwards.

- **Because sharks grow slowly** and don't bear many young, it is especially hard for a species to build up its numbers again after being overfished.

- **As predators**, sharks are at the top of the food chain. Poisonous chemicals from pollution collect in sea creatures, and when sharks eat their prey, the poison builds up in their bodies. Scientists think this may make some sharks ill and make it harder for them to reproduce.

... FASCINATING FACT ...
Many shark species are so hard to study that scientists have no idea
how many of them are left in the sea.

Endangered species

- **An endangered species** is in danger of dying out and becoming extinct.

- **When a species becomes extinct**, all the members of that species die and it can never exist again.

- **Scientists try to find** out if a shark species is at risk by counting how many sharks are seen in a particular area and measuring how much this changes over time.

- **For example**, experts found that sandbar shark sightings on America's east coast fell by 20 percent between the 1970s and the 1990s. The sandbar shark is now an endangered shark.

- **International organizations** such as the IUCN (International Union for the Conservation of Nature and Natural Resources) compile lists of which species are endangered.

- **According to the IUCN** over 50 shark species are now endangered.

- **Well-known sharks** that are endangered include great white, whale and basking sharks.

- **Most sharks** have become endangered because of overfishing (see sharks in trouble).

- **Some sharks and shark relatives**, such as leopard sharks and sawfish, are threatened when natural coastlines and estuaries are developed and built on, for example to build tourist resorts. This destroys nursery areas where sharks lay eggs or bear their young.

- **The Ganges shark**, which is found in the river Ganges in India, is one of the most endangered sharks.

▲ *Great whites are one species that are known to be in danger of dying out. There are several international campaigns to try to save them.*

Saving sharks

- **Since scientists realized** that some sharks were becoming endangered, governments and wildlife have started working to try to save them.

- **Ecotourism helps** to save sharks, as long as it's managed carefully. It encourages local people not to kill sharks, as they can make more money from them as tourist attractions than they can by fishing for them.

▼ *Scientists have noticed that some types of sharks take an active interest in diving cages. They seem to become more tame the more encounters they have with humans.*

- **Some shark-fishing countries**, such as the USA and Australia, have imposed quotas to limit how many of each type of shark their fishermen can catch.

- **Governments** can also ban the killing of particular sharks altogether. For example, the UK has passed a law making it illegal to catch or disturb a basking shark.

- **Some countries** have set up marine wildlife reserves where harming wildlife is banned. They operate in places such as Tasmania to protect shark nursery areas along the coast.

- **Conservation charities** such as WWF (The WorldWide Fund for Nature) work to educate people who encounter sharks, such as fishermen, to help them avoid killing sharks unnecessarily.

- **By banning trade** in shark products, governments can stop some people from killing sharks.

- **To help protect** sharks, people should avoid buying products such as shark's-fin soup and shark jawbones that are sold in some tourist resorts.

- **Some shark charities** will let you 'adopt' a shark. You pay a fee and receive information about a particular shark living in a protected area. The money goes towards conservation campaigns.

...FASCINATING FACT...
Some scientists are worried that diving with sharks makes them less scared of humans, which could put sharks at greater risk.

Shark myths and legends

▲ *A 17th-century engraving showing the Biblical prophet Jonah and the 'great fish' that swallowed him whole – which could have been either a shark or a whale.*

● **There are many** myths and legends involving sharks. Most of them come from parts of the world where sharks are common.

● **Hawaiian legends** tell of a shark king, Kamo Hoa Lii, and a shark queen, Ka'ahu, who controlled all the other sharks in the sea.

- **In one Hawaiian myth**, a minor god named Maui threw a shark into the sky, where it formed patterns of stars that can still be seen today.

- **In a similar legend** of the Warrau people of South America, a man arranged for his mother-in-law to be eaten by a shark. As a punishment his own leg was bitten off and became the constellation known today as Orion's Belt.

- **Another Hawaiian story** tells how a shark king fell in love with a human woman. He took a human shape, came ashore and married her, and they had a son. The shark king ordered that the boy should never eat meat, but he did, and immediately found he could turn himself into a shark.

- **The Christian holy book**, the Bible, tells how the prophet Jonah was swallowed by a 'great fish'. In modern translations this is called a whale, but some people think it might have meant a shark.

- **The ancient Greek writer** Aristotle developed a theory that sharks had to roll upside-down in order to bite. This isn't true, but the myth lived on for centuries.

- **In legends from the South Pacific**, 'shark men' were sharks that could take human form and come ashore to cause mischief and steal things.

- **Old Japanese legends** also featured a terrifying god called the shark man.

> ...FASCINATING FACT...
> When China and Japan were fighting each other in the
> Second World War, the Chinese painted sharks on their
> fighter planes to try to scare the Japanese.

Shark beliefs and folklore

- **Throughout history**, people – especially sailors – have believed all sorts of amazing things about sharks. Many unproved shark beliefs still survive to this day.

- **Sailors used to say** sharks could smell a dead body and followed a ship if someone on board had died. Scientists today think there may actually be some truth in this.

- **Sailors also** used to believe that sharks liked eating humans and would go out of their way to find them. In fact, this isn't true at all.

- **In the past**, many peoples around the world worshipped shark gods – especially people who depended on fishing for their living.

- **People from the Solomon Islands**, in the Pacific Ocean, believed that the spirits of people who had died lived on in sharks.

- **The Solomon Islanders** even used to make human sacrifices to sharks to keep the shark-spirits happy.

- **In Vietnam**, the whale shark is known as Ca ong or 'Sir Fish'. This shark was once worshipped there and there are still ancient shrines to it along the Vietnamese coast today.

- **Because sharks rarely** get diseases such as cancer, many people believe eating shark products, especially shark cartilage, can protect against cancer. So far, there is no scientific evidence for this.

- **In Fiji** in the Pacific Ocean, people used to catch sharks, roll them onto their backs, and kiss their stomachs. This was believed to make the sharks harmless, so that people could fish safely.

▲ *The coastline of the Pacific island of Fiji. Sharks are common in the shallow waters here and the Fijians have many traditional beliefs and customs relating to sharks.*

···FASCINATING FACT···
In Europe, catching a shark used to be considered good luck, especially if it was female.

Sharks in art, books and films

- **Ancient peoples** often made images of sharks. For example, Maori and Inuit artists made carvings of sharks from wood and bone.

- **Ancient aboriginal** rock art depict sharks along with other animals that were important to the early Aborigines such as turtles and seabirds.

- **In 1778**, American artist John Singleton Copley painted a famous picture of Brook Watson being attacked by a shark (see survival stories).

- **In his 1851 novel** *Moby Dick*, Herman Melville described a character named Queequeg almost losing his hand to a shark, even though it had been killed and dragged on board.

- **Another famous novel**, *20,000 Leagues Under the Sea* by Jules Verne, features man-eating sharks.

- **The best-known shark novel** of all is *Jaws*, by Peter Benchley, published in 1974. It tells a story of a great white shark attacking swimmers off the east coast off the USA.

- **In 1975**, *Jaws* was made into a film by Steven Spielberg. It broke box-office records and is still one of the biggest-grossing films of all time.

- **Much of *Jaws*** was filmed using a 7 m-long artificial shark, known as Bruce.

- **There were three film sequels** to *Jaws*, including a 3D version. The audience wore special 3D spectacles that made the shark appear to come out of the screen towards them.

- **In a later shark movie**, *Deep Blue Sea* (1999), the shark sequences were partly created using computer animation.

◀ *A still from the famous shark film* Deep Blue Sea. *It tells the story of a group of scientists who use genetic engineering to create super-intelligent sharks – which then turn against their captors.*

Shark science

▲ *A manager and a marine biologist (sealife scientist) in a German aquarium, counting the different types of sharks in their shark tank. They are in an underwater tunnel that allows scientists and tourists to observe the sharks closely.*

- **Sharks are among** the least-understood animals on Earth. Scientists around the world are trying to find out more about them.

- **The study of sharks** is sometimes called elasmobranchology.

- **Knowing more about sharks** – things such as how they breed and what they need to survive – will help us to conserve them and stop shark species from dying out.

- **To find out how sharks live**, scientists have to study them in the wild. This is called 'fieldwork'.

- **Scientists also catch sharks** so they can study them in captivity. This lets them look closely at how sharks swim, eat, breed and behave in other ways.

- **In laboratories**, scientists study things such as sharks' blood, skin and cartilage to find out how their bodies work.

- **Some scientists** study sharks' cells to try to find out why they get so few diseases. This information could help to make new medicines.

- **In aquariums**, scientists test sharks' reactions to see how their brains and senses work.

- **Governments** and wildlife charities sometimes pay scientists to study sharks.

...FASCINATING FACT...
After scientists found out how sharks' denticles reduced drag, a swimming costume company designed a swimming costume that worked in the same way.

Shark scientists

- **There are many different types** of scientists who work with sharks.

- **Biologists** are scientists who study living things. Many shark scientists are marine biologists – which means they study sea life.

- **Zoologists** are scientists who study animals, and ichthyologists are scientists who study fish. These scientists sometimes work with sharks.

- **Other shark scientists** study shark genes and DNA – the instructions inside cells that make their bodies work. Scientists who study genes and DNA are called geneticists.

- **Paleontologists** study fossils, and shark fossils are very important in revealing how sharks evolved. There are scientists who specialize in studying just shark fossils.

- **Oceanographers** study the sea. They know all about shark habitats and how sharks live together with other animals.

- **Most shark scientists** work for universities or research centres such as the Woods Hole Oceanographic Institute in Massachusetts, USA.

- **The famous French** undersea expert Jacques Cousteau was one of the first people to study sharks underwater. He invented scuba diving gear, which scientists still use when studying sharks.

- **One of today's** most famous shark scientists is American zoologist Dr. Eugenie Clark. She has studied shark behaviour and deep-sea sharks.

- **If you'd like** to be a shark scientist, it will help if you pick subjects such as biology and chemistry at school, and study biology or zoology at university.

▶ *This diver is wearing the latest diving equipment. This allows scientists to study sharks close-up in their natural habitats.*

Studying sharks

- **To learn more about sharks**, scientists need ways of finding, following and catching them.

- **Most shark scientists** have to be physically strong and good at diving.

- **Scientists** often use diving cages or protective chainmail suits to get close to sharks.

- **They can also study** sharks such as great whites without going in the water, using cameras on the ends of long poles.

- **To follow sharks**, scientists radio-track them. They catch a shark and attach a transmitter that gives out radio signals. Wherever the shark goes, they can pick up the signals and plot the shark's location on a map.

- **Scientists tag sharks** by attaching a special collar or tag saying where and when the shark was last seen. The same shark may then be found again somewhere else, giving scientists clues about shark movements and migrations.

- **Scientists have invented a camera** that can be attached to a shark to record a shark's-eye view of its travels. After a while, the strap holding the camera dissolves, and it floats to the surface where it can be collected.

- **To tag or track a shark**, scientists have to catch it using a net or trap. They may drug it so that they can attach the transmitter or tag safely.

- **Some shark science** involves dissecting dead sharks – to find out how their bodies work or what they have eaten recently.

- **Scientists have to be careful** when working with live sharks. Just like fishermen who handle sharks, they may get bitten by a shark that is not happy about being caught.

▲ *These scientists have caught a small lemon shark. Holding it in the water so that it can breathe, they are measuring it and attaching a tag to its dorsal fin, so that they'll know if they catch the same shark again.*

Early sharks

- **Sharks first evolved** about 380 million years ago. That means they were around long before the dinosaurs.

- **Sharks' basic body shapes** and behaviour have hardly changed since they first appeared.

- **Experts think sharks** evolved from ancient types of fish that had no jawbones.

- **Sharks appeared** long before many other kinds of fish that are alive today, such as salmon and goldfish.

- **One of the earliest sharks** of all was *Cladoselache*, which lived 370 million years ago. It was around 1.5 m long, and had 3-pointed teeth, just as frilled sharks do now.

- *Stethacanthus*, which lived about 350 million years ago, was a strange-looking shark with a platform of denticles on top of its first dorsal fin.

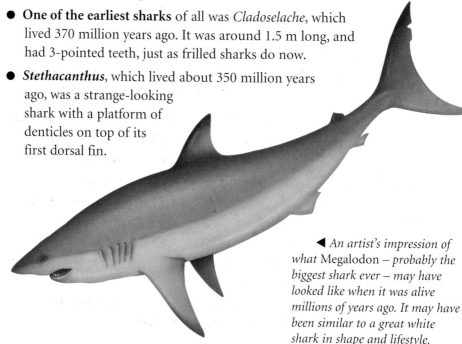

◀ *An artist's impression of what* Megalodon – *probably the biggest shark ever – may have looked like when it was alive millions of years ago. It may have been similar to a great white shark in shape and lifestyle.*

◄ A fossilized Megalodon *tooth (left) compared to a tooth from a modern great white shark. They are similar in shape and sharpness, but the* Megalodon *tooth is much bigger.*

● *Hybodus* **lived** about 160 million years ago. Like many modern sharks, it had both sharp cutting teeth and flat, blunt, chewing teeth.

● **The biggest shark** ever was probably *Megalodon*. It first appeared about 20 million years ago. Scientists think it looked like a great white shark, only bigger –maybe 20 m in length (as long as two buses).

● **Of course,** these prehistoric sharks didn't have these names when they were alive, as there were no humans around to name them. Their names have been given to them by modern scientists.

● **Sharks survived** a huge mass extinction 65 million years ago, which wiped out other creatures such as dinosaurs and ammonites.

Shark fossils

▶ *Fossils of sharks' teeth are much more common than other shark fossils. This is partly because sharks lose hundreds of teeth in their lifetime and form fossils by themselves. It's also because teeth are among the hardest parts of a shark's body.*

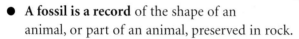

- **A fossil is a record** of the shape of an animal, or part of an animal, preserved in rock.

- **A fossil forms** when an animal dies and is gradually covered by sand or mud. Over a very long time, the sand or mud hardens into rock. The animal rots away, but its shape is left behind, and may get filled in with minerals to leave a 'model' of the animal.

- **Often**, only the hardest parts of an animal, such as its skeleton, get fossilized.

- **Because sharks** have cartilage skeletons, which are softer than bone, there are very few complete shark fossils. Many shark fossils only show teeth or fins.

- **Scientists use shark fossils** to find out what sharks looked like long ago and how they lived. They often use tooth fossils to guess how big an entire shark was.

- **Shark fossils** are often found on land in places that used to be seas millions of years ago.

- **Some of the best** shark fossil-finding areas are in parts of the USA, such as California, Maryland and Oklahoma. One hill in California is called Sharktooth Hill because there are so many shark fossils there.

- **Palaeontologists** go searching for fossils at good sites and dig, cut or chip them out of the surrounding rocks. Then they take them back to a lab to clean them and study them carefully.

- **Fossils show** that some sharks that are alive today, such as horn sharks and catsharks, are very similar to ones that lived millions of years ago.

- **Fossils** are often on display at many museums and fossil shops.

▼ *A group of palaeontologists at work. They have to be very careful when they dig precious and delicate fossils out of the ground. Detailed notes record all their findings.*

Shark discoveries and mysteries

▶ *A whale shark living in an aquarium opens its mouth to be fed by its keeper. Like many sharks, whale sharks are mysterious and scientists know very little about them. Keeping them in captivity can help them find out more.*

● **Shark scientists** are still finding out new things about sharks, and puzzling over unanswered questions.

● **Shark experts** sometimes disagree strongly about shark facts. They meet up at conferences where they share their discoveries and hold debates.

- **For example**, some experts think the prehistoric shark *Megalodon* died out over a million years ago, while others say it lived until 10,000 years ago.

- **There is also a mystery** about why basking sharks seem to disappear at certain times of year.

- **The dwarf lanternshark** was only discovered in 1985 and new species of sharks are still being found.

- **Scientists** don't always find new shark species in the sea. Instead, they are often found in fish markets or reported by local people.

- **In 2004**, scientists looked inside Greenland sharks' stomachs and found they eat giant and colossal squid. Before this, only sperm whales were thought to eat these creatures.

- **In 2002**, scientists worked out how to test the DNA in shark's-fin soup to see which species it was made from. This helps to stop people hunting protected sharks.

- **Also in 2002**, scientists studying whale sharks found that they don't just eat plankton. Sometimes they wait for other fish to lay their eggs so that they can eat them.

- **Scientists studying shark's fins** in 2001 found they sometimes contain very high levels of the poison mercury, which comes from from pollution in seawater.

Shark records

◄ *A face-to-face encounter with the aptly named bigeye thresher shark, owner of the biggest eyes for its size in the shark world.*

- **The most widespread shark** is the blue shark, which is found in most of the world's seas and oceans.

- **The brightest** luminescent shark is the cookie-cutter. Its glow is as bright as a reading lamp.

- **More than ten shark** species share the title of rarest shark, as they are known from only one specimen. They include two types of angel shark, the Taiwan angel shark and the ocellated angel shark.

- **The flattest-bodied** sharks are angel and wobbegong sharks.

- **The bigeye thresher shark** has bigger eyes in relation to its body size than any other shark.

- **The shortfin mako** makes the highest leaps. It can jump more than 5 m out of the water.

- **The whale shark** has the most pups at once – up to 300.
- **The fussiest eaters** in the shark world are bullhead sharks. Some will only eat sea urchins.
- **The common thresher shark** has the longest tail compared to its body size.
- **The great white shark** has had more books written and films made about it than any other shark.

▲ *A great white, the top shark record-holder. It's the world's best-known, deadliest and most popular shark.*

Index

Index

Index

Acknowledgements

The publishers would like to thank the following artists
who have contributed to this book:

John Butler, Jim Channel, Luigi Galante, Colin Howard (Advocate Art),
Andrea Morandi, Mike Saunders, Rudi Vizi, Mike White (Temple Rogers)

The publishers would like to thank the following sources
for the use of their photographs:

Page 84 AFP/Getty Images; 141 Lawson Wood/Corbis;
160 Universal/pictorialpress.com; 164 Jeffrey L Rotman/Corbis;
166 AFP/Getty Images; 170 Bob Care/AFP/Getty Images;
172 Kevin Fleming/Corbis; 174 Peter Parks/AFP/Getty Images;
180 Toshifumi Kitamura/AFP/Getty Images; 182 Jay Directo/AFP/Getty Images;
188 Philip Spruvt/Stapleton Collection/Corbis; 193 Warner/pictorialpress.com;
194 Kay Nietfeld/AFP/Getty Images; 198 Jeffrey L Rotman/Corbis;
204 Toru Yamanaka/AFP/Getty Images; 206 Jeffrey L Rotman/Corbis

All other photographs from Miles Kelly Archives
Corel, digitalvision, Hemera